Honyocker Dreams

Honyocker Dreams

Montana Memories

David Mogen

University of Nebraska Press
Lincoln & London

Publication of this volume was
assisted by The Virginia Faulkner
Fund, established in memory of
Virginia Faulkner, editor in chief of the
University of Nebraska Press.

Library of Congress Cataloging-in-
Publication Data
Mogen, David, 1945–
Honyocker dreams: Montana memories
/ David Mogen.
p. cm.
Includes bibliographical references.
ISBN 978-0-8032-2518-3 (cloth: alk.
paper)
1. Mogen, David, 1945– —Childhood
and youth. 2. Montana—Biography.
3. Montana—Social life and customs.
I. Title.

CT275.M59437A3 2011
978.6'033092—dc22
[B]
2010022915

Set in Sabon.

In memory of my parents, Harold and Thelma

Honyockers! I don't know where the word comes from. The *Harvard Dictionary of Regional English* says that it may be a blend of "Hunk" (for Hungarian) and "Polack," but that sounds like a grope in the dark. What it effectively does is to travesty the word *homesteader* syllable by syllable, and render the homesteaders themselves as ridiculous oafs, saps, dimwits. It gathers up all the anger and contempt that the ranchers felt for the newcomers and squeezes them together into a sound a man might make when delivering a gob into a spittoon. *Hon-yockers!* The fence builders took much of the sting out of the word by adopting it for themselves. The hostility of the ranchers helped to sharpen the honyockers' sense of community.

—JONATHAN RABAN, *Bad Land: An American Romance*

What the heck is a "Honyocker"? . . . Well, after hours of exhaustive Google research, I came up with the following tidbits to try and define the elusive HONYOCKER:

In standard German the word "Huhn-jager" means hen-hunter.

In the Czech language a honyocker is hunyad, which comes from hunac and means a shaggy fellow.

In the Hungarian dictionary it is spelled Hanyag and han-yak and means negligent, careless, sloppy, or forgetful.

In the early 1900s the ranchers in Montana did not like the homesteaders (dirt farmers) who broke up the native prairie and called them honyockers, which is a degrading cowboy slang word.

One person said white homesteaders who settled Indian land west of Mobridge, SD, were called honyockers.

. . . my personal favorite—that which I strive to be:

In North Dakota and surrounding states honyocker is often taken to mean a backward, old-fashioned type of rural person.

—From the website www.Honyocker.org
(accessed March 18, 2006)

Contents

Acknowledgments

Most fundamentally, this book attempts to reconstruct two eras that have passed—primarily the postwar small-town Montana world of my own childhood and, more speculatively, the Montana homesteading frontier world in which my parents and their pioneer ancestors grew up. The sources for such imaginative reconstructions are too various to be fully acknowledged, but I'd like to pay tribute to some I consider most important.

This is a memoir, not a history, so while it is true to my own memories of places, people, and events, I'm aware that other observers and participants might remember them differently. I have altered names of those who are not family members or close friends to avoid entangling others unnecessarily (or perhaps inaccurately from their points of view) in my own stories.

My most direct sources, of course, are the members of my immediate family, all of whom have played roles in constructing my book as well as my life. My parents' stories weave throughout the book, and my younger brothers and sisters—Phil, Doris, Mike, Kirk, and Helen—all contributed to sorting out our family stories.

Extended family members, some of whom appear in these pages as well, helped me to shape and recover these stories. To reconstruct the ranching history of my father's family, my cousin Ron Mogen and his wife, Pat, have provided invaluable information, both in the form of family and local history documents and through their conversation and hospitality so generously extended during my visits to their home in Forsyth.

My Blackfeet relatives also appear in several of these stories. I'm especially grateful to my late great-uncle Gene Ground (who passed away during the writing of this book) and to my cousin Mary Ellen LaFramboise and her husband, Conrad, for their warm hospitality and insight. Getting to know them has enriched my understanding of our family history and Montana heritage.

Thanks as well for the hospitality and assistance of my relatives from the Plentywood area: Aunt Ruth, Uncle Louie and Aunt Margaret, as well as my cousins Duane and Valerie all helped me to reconstruct the pioneer world in northeastern Montana, where my mother grew up.

Numerous writers and colleagues have provided important feedback while this manuscript has evolved. Gerry Callahan, science writer and fellow collaborator on numerous interdisciplinary and creative writing projects, has provided feedback over the years while my early stories developed into a book. I'd like especially to thank the other members of my old writing group here in Fort Collins, all of whom originally helped me see how my Montana stories were beginning to form a larger narrative: John Calderazzo, SueEllen Campbell, Pattie Cowell, Mark Fiege, Sue Doe, and Gina Callahan. Fiction writer Judy Doenges provided feedback on an early version of the manuscript. Bill Bevis, from the University of Montana at Missoula, provided important feedback on some early stories, and his colleague Nancy Cook's knowledgeable advice and perceptive editing helped me tighten up and restructure the final manuscript.

Laura Pritchett and Steve Church, two of my ex-students who have become established authors themselves, provided encouragement and guidance at an important stage of the book's development, as did my Irish linguist colleague, Gerry Delahunty. Two friends from my graduate schools days in

Boulder, Ray Hogler and Martie Faulk, both authors now themselves, shared their perspectives as new readers of the final manuscript. Mary Crow, poet laureate of Colorado for many years, advised me on some of my final revisions.

Several colleagues from the Western Literature Association have provided me encouragement and advice over the years, originally simply by appreciating and often laughing with me about my stories of growing up on the Montana Hi-Line. Without the support of friends such as Alan Weltzien, Bonnie MacDonald, David Fenimore, Nancy Cook, Mark Busby, Steve Cook, Drucilla Wall, and Sue Maher I might never have conceived of writing these stories down. My editorial consultant, LaurieAnn Ray, designed the first draft of "A Honyocker's Map of Montana" and a concept for the cover, and she also formatted the final manuscript for the University of Nebraska Press. Cathy Byron, another relative from the ranching side of my family, created a link on her website for the Lynch-Callan Reunion in 2009, which allowed me to inform the extensive family network—descendants of the eight daughters and son of my Irish great-great-grandparents—about what was then a forthcoming book.

I'd like to thank two editors for encouragement and advice that made this book possible. Dawn Marano showed me how my earlier collection of reflective essays was evolving into a larger narrative. And as I told Ladette Randolph after I finished my major revision of my first draft, "You helped me discover how to write the book I'd dreamed of writing."

Finally I'd like to thank my wife, Liz, first reader and final editor of all of these stories, for her loving support and advice. I'm grateful to her, and to all those over the years who have helped me to believe in and express these honyocker dreams.

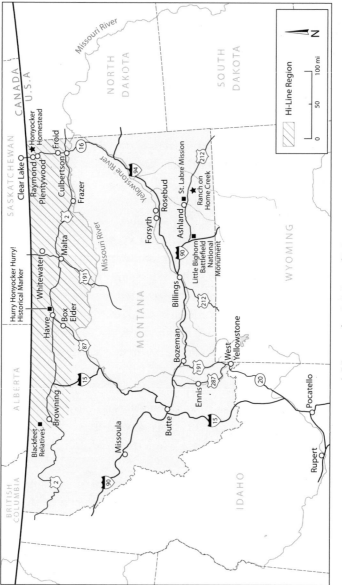

A Honyocker's Map of Montana

Endings and Beginnings

Riding the Yellowstone Trail

Without father, without mother, without descent, having neither beginning of days, nor end of life . . .

—HEBREWS 7:3

Play the drum slowly, and play the fife lowly,
Play the dead march as you carry me along.

—"The Dying Cowboy"

This is how it ended.

He's telling the story of his life, I realize, about the time we pass Big Timber.

Mom strains to hear from the back seat. He's speaking to us but his eyes roam the landscape as he speaks.

"*I've been down this road a few times,*" he begins. I've just merged into the traffic on I-90 west of Billings, heading back for the last time to my parents' home outside of Rupert, Idaho, in the Snake River valley. "*It used to be old Highway 10, before they built the interstate. Before that, when we first got cars, it was a gravel road we still called the Yellowstone Trail, from the old horse and wagon trails that followed the river.*"

I'm still adjusting to driving his car, to the smooth hushed glide of the automatic transmission and riding low on the highway, rather than shifting gears with the high view from my four-wheel-drive Nissan Frontier truck; still feeling a bit awkward and preoccupied. But something in the way he speaks triggers a vision of his long life on the road, a Montana school superintendent driving to and from our homes in small towns along the eastern Hi-Line. He's back now on this last trip traveling through this southeastern Montana country of his earliest memories. Beginning his last journey brings back memories of when he first left home, riding this Yellowstone Trail from the old ranch to the wider world.

So now it's the three of us making the final trip to their Idaho home. And the big-cell squamous cancer, it turns out, that he carries in his hip, that actually came from his lungs, that has metastasized so that his condition is irreversible. His visit to the clinic in Billings has turned into his last stop, while my youngest brother, Kirk, and his family have moved into a ranch house under the rimrocks big enough for all of them and visiting family during his final months. The doctors give him six months to a year, an imprecise yet unalterable death sentence, imposed by the invisible executioner that rides with us in his bone marrow as he speaks.

We all know that this is his last road trip, riding in the passenger seat of his car that he can no longer drive. He scans the familiar landscapes as the stories weave together. At first I think he's just making conversation, but now he's settled into a rhythm I've not heard before. His eyes absorb the scenery as his voice slides into the past.

Columbus, where your brother Phil was born just fourteen months after you. See that turnoff? I guess you've never been back to that little cabin outside of Park City we shared with your aunt Roma and uncle Phil and your cousin Jackie after the war, while they were still building the married student housing in Bozeman for all of us veterans there on the G.I. Bill. That first semester I lived in the Quonset huts they put up for us while they finished the strip-housing. I'd ride this road weekends and whenever else I could to see your mom and you two little guys. When they finished that married student housing we finally all lived together there in Bozeman. But that's where our first Montana home was, about eight miles down this road.

This landscape is filled with stories, I realize, as we glide by the exit to Columbus that I'd passed dozens of times without a second thought. I know Phil was born there, but I've never imagined the full story. For the first time I visualize what an exciting and vivid time that must have been for all of them, just reunited after the long ordeal of the war, Mom and her younger sister Roma back with their husbands and now with new babies, all living together in their first home. I hadn't realized that Dad spent that first term living in Quonset hut housing with the other newly returned veterans, driving back from Bozeman on weekends up and down this Yellowstone River valley to be with his new family.

Now his voice drifts back in time and space to the old ranch on Home Creek, just east of the Tongue River by the Custer National Forest, where he grew up.

I've seen a lot of changes in my life. When I grew up that Ashland country was still horse country, like it was in the nineteenth-century. Then we got cars, then the big freeways. And now everybody travels by jet.

Life was tough back then, I guess, but we didn't know any better. We kids would ride five miles on horseback in dead winter to that little school in Willow Crossing, then get our frozen hands beaten with a ruler if we were late. Christ, to-day if someone sent little kids out on horseback in weather like that they'd have them taken away because of neglect and abuse. But that was just the way it was, and nobody thought twice about it.

This was just one of those stories emblazoned in my memory from childhood that fascinated and transfixed me, about the teacher beating the stiff hands of children who arrived at school half-frozen after riding through a snowstorm. How could you complain about anything that happened at school after hearing a story like that? And how could you complain about anything after hearing the story of the sickly younger sister for whom the doctor prescribed an orange a day, who only got one section each morning because that was all her family could afford, while the older brothers and sisters looked on with longing?

Stories that spoke of hardship yet captured my imagination. Starting the day at the age of six by riding miles on horseback to school, savoring an orange as a special treat indulged in only at Christmas time, unless you were specially blessed with illness. Tough times, but filled with passion and challenges. I had never actually spent much time around horses, so my visions of these old days were shaped by books and movies as well as by my parents' words. But part of me had always envied kids who started and ended the school day by riding through countryside on horseback, rather than just trudging back and forth up the street to school.

Mostly, men and women had different jobs back then. None of the girls in my family ever milked a cow or did outside work. And we men never did anything in the home. I re-

ally can't remember when Bob and I started working. On a family spread like ours there was usually just Dad and Mom and us kids to do the work, and there was no end to work. I milked cows about as early as I can remember. That could be a tough job on cold mornings, especially when you didn't even have a stall to stand them in. You'd just sidle up to them with your bucket out in the corral and try to keep them still until the job was done. But it sure gave you strong hands in a hurry.

I remember our trip to the old ranch house by Home Creek.

I tramp through the dried manure now covering the dirt floors, as Dad and his older brother, Uncle Bob, and his elderly cowboy uncle, Brian Tucker, pace around inside swapping stories. It seems too small for seven people, I marvel, as they explain how at night cloth drapes could be drawn to separate the kitchen from the main bed and the small kids' bedroom to the side.

"God, remember the time Dad caught us in there trying to smoke dried weeds in that old pipe we'd found?" recalls Uncle Bob, as we look down into the root cellar just west of the cabin. "I thought we were in big trouble, but he just shook his head and said, 'You boys better come up from there before you burn something down or make yourselves sick.'"

I gaze over at the small barn and corral, imagining my dad as a young boy on a wintry morning trying to get a cow to stay still, while his hands direct steaming streams of milk that make metallic music in the cold bucket.

I left home in 1934 when I was fourteen. Worked my way through three years of high school there at the St. Labre Mis-

sion set up for the Cheyenne, but when they closed the high school to white kids I went back to work on the family ranch because Dad was sick, then went back and cowboyed full-time at the Mission until I saved some money so I could finish high school at Rosebud. I had two-hundred dollars then and bought the first suit I ever owned to wear at graduation. That would be 1939, when I was nineteen.

Dad and my uncles point out the graves of my great-great-grandparents Patrick and Margaret Lynch, according to them the first white couple buried in the cemetery. They're showing us St. Labre Mission, in Ashland, just east of the Northern Cheyenne Reservation, several miles north and west of the Home Creek ranch. Back when Dad was a kid this was the center of civilization for the local Irish in the ranching community, at least, and an outpost where the Cheyenne could try to figure out how to survive in the new world that had surrounded them.

Snatches of Dad's stories I'd grown up with are now coming back, from his respectful memories of Father Dan's Latin class, to the severe lectures the nuns gave to the girls about the dangers of overly polished shoes that might reflect their underwear to the boys' leering eyes. And then there was the initiation story that intrigued but disturbed me, when he and a group of other boys met a new student at the train, after which Dad, because of his skill in boxing, was assigned the job of fighting him, before the others rubbed down his bruised face with horse liniment.

Well, welcome to the Mission, I thought, thankful that I'd never encountered testing that organized and ruthless in new towns while I was growing up. I noticed the tinge of

regret that entered Dad's voice as he realized the cruelty of
an anecdote he'd apparently intended just as an example of
humorous horseplay.

And I'd never before understood that he'd spent that year
working at the ranch then cowboying at the Mission, before
he moved to Rosebud to finish high school. In his description of that first suit I heard his satisfaction at preparing to
enter the larger world on his own.

*The toughest years were back in the thirties, when the price
of beef dropped so much it cost us as much as we'd get paid
to ship our cattle to Chicago. Then came the drought and
the godawful locusts, swarming over everything, rolling in
like clouds. After watching those poor cattle die of drought
and poor feed I never really wanted to go back to that ranching life. By the time Dad offered to turn it over to me after
the war I just wasn't interested. I wanted to go to medical
school or teach, and that's what I did.*

We kids grew up with stories of the Depression, but now I
suddenly realize how radically those times altered Dad's life,
and the lives of our family. What if he had taken the ranch
and we had grown up grounded in that particular piece of
land by Home Creek, where the family history extended back
almost a century, instead of moving from town to town along
the Hi-Line, always the kids of the new teacher or superintendent? How would our lives have been changed? And what a
sad ending to Grandpa Slim's cowboy homesteader dreams,
I reflected, to realize that none of his children wanted to ex-
tend them into the future.

As we pass the sign for Big Timber Dad describes his first
major journey up this Yellowstone River valley, when he left

the old home in southeastern Montana to seek his fortunes in the legendary hayfields of the Big Hole.

After graduating from high school I cruised from job to job, working my way west up this Yellowstone valley. Spent some time harvesting spuds with old Les Dunning. We made a hell of a spud crew. Then came over here to Big Timber to do some haying, until I heard about the really big spreads over in the Big Hole valley, so I headed west again. Got the best job I'd ever had, working on a big crew for three dollars a day, which was top wages then. It was the first job I'd had where you didn't have to get up to milk cows and wrangle horses before the real work started.

So I was doing great, but then I got this weird swelling. Phlebitis, it turned out. They punctured it and this horrible smelling pus oozed out. But then it came back. I ended up in a hospital in Dillon for three months, the longest rest I'd ever had. Turned out the ranch was big enough that they were under a worker's comp program, so I got all my medical expenses paid, plus two dollars a day while I was in there. That was a hell of a deal.

I'd just turned fifty-two and had now been married ten years while Liz and I had reconstructed our historic old home into something special and comfortable. I'd been tenured and promoted and had lived in Fort Collins longer than I'd ever lived in any one place. I was feeling pretty secure and content, with a sabbatical just under way and time finally to write and read, feeling like maybe I'd gotten most of the big things about figured out, when cancer suddenly turned the life of me and everyone close to me upside down. I was fifty-two and the oldest of six and I realized that I'd never dealt with death this close, except through Liz, whose father died

suddenly nine months after our wedding. But that was unexpected and over, a sudden shock of grief, though it took
her years to heal.

Now I was living with dying for the first time, hearing it
in my father's voice as he surveyed his life through the landscape. I heard him taking stock of what he'd seen and what
he'd thought. Sorting out the things that matter. Beginning
to say goodbye to places before returning to his youngest
son's new home, where he would say goodbye to friends and
family as his life ebbed away.

We're south of Bozeman now, following the Gallatin River
down to West Yellowstone, one of my favorite drives during my summer fly-fishing trips. But I've never been over it
this late in the year, watching the yellow aspen leaves drifting in the ice-fringed river. Dad has been describing the milk
truck deliveries he made while we lived in Bozeman, when
he'd get up at four in the morning to drive his route to Three
Forks and back before his classes began. I'm trying to determine whether I really remember the time he took me along
when I was two or whether I'm just constructing a fantasy
about it based on his story. But he falls silent as a late October snow flurry sweeps in on the pass, slowing us down
while weaving headlights appear and fade away in the dancing flakes, until we finally burst back into full sunlight bright
on the new snow that swathes the river. Now he's reflecting about the differences between his own ranching culture
and Mom's farming communities, and there's a bitter edge
to some of his memories I hadn't noticed before.

*Where I grew up was real different than northeastern Mon-
tana, where your mom was from. We were ranching people,*

self-made individualists, Republicans. It damn near killed Dad to admit that some of FDR's programs helped us survive. In your mom's country people were farmers, mostly Democrats.

Down in that Ashland country the big ranchers called the shots. Nobody in state or county government would mess with them. They'd squash them like bugs if they did. And most people around there would follow their lead. Dad's ranch was mortgaged to one of them. Everyone admired them for being successful. They'd have the contracts for grazing cattle in Custer National Forest locked up and no one would ever try to count how many cattle they actually ran. They'd sell more cattle every year than they paid taxes on, and everyone knew it.

There were a lot of good things about that old ranching country though. We had a strong code of hospitality. In the early days you could pull in anyplace to get a meal or two and a place to stay. If nobody was home you helped yourself to what was there. If they were, they'd find a place somewhere for you to throw out a bedroll and sleep. During the winter cowboys would ride the grub line. Just show up at your door and work anywhere from a few days to a few weeks for board and room, then move on down the line. When we had company us four older kids would just sleep in one bed. Bob and I faced one direction, and Marie and Clara faced the other. Nobody had their own bed back then.

We pull into West Yellowstone late that afternoon. Now that tourist season has ended it's practically a ghost town about to hibernate for the winter, so we have our pick of motels that are preparing to shut down until spring. I've never been here when it wasn't swarming with tourists, and I realize that arriving in West Yellowstone has been part of a ritual I've loved that now, suddenly, is finished.

Every spring I'd turn in final grades, exhausted mentally and physically from editing and grading piles of term papers and final exams, then load the truck with fishing and camping gear. I traveled solo because Liz liked to relax and work around the yard after finishing her term. Spend the first night fishing in Saratoga, Wyoming, and soaking in the hottest mineral water hobo pool in the West before heading northwest on Highway 287 through Wind River country to the Tetons. Drive through Yellowstone Park before the summer traffic got impossible, arriving at West Yellowstone for dinner in what was already a carnival of tourists from everywhere on earth. Scout out the fishing news for the Madison and Hebgen Lake and Henry's Lake in the crowded fly store before setting up camp by the river, then drive a few days later to my parents' Idaho home for my annual spring visit. Walk with Dad through his garden the size of a small truck farm before eating roast beef and mashed potatoes and gravy and grouselot (Mom's German cabbage salad) and fresh-made apple pie. Kick back in a lawn chair to read in the orchard that their backyard has become since we first planted the sapling trees when they moved there in the mid-seventies.

So now I realize that I'm arriving in West Yellowstone from the wrong direction at the wrong time of year on our way to sell the Idaho home and end my ritual forever.

It's strange to have a western tourist playpen all to ourselves. I walk the empty streets scouting out restaurants and decide on the Robbers Roost, which is a fine steakhouse with a view of the town, but I realize too late that I hadn't anticipated the problem presented by the stairs. The doctors had warned us that Dad's hip is so fragile that it could break with any collision, and if he steps wrong and jolts it he freezes with pain. By the time we get up the stairs he's pale and shaky. I remember the doctors' misgivings about him taking the trip, and when he limps off to the bathroom Mom tells me she's worried about how he's going to survive the next week.

But by next afternoon we're caught up in the whirlwind of their last visit to Rupert and the Idaho home. Meeting with the lawyer to go over the will with me and arrange for transfers of power of attorney when they become necessary. Meeting with representatives in the local bank to go over accounts and arrange to transfer funds to Billings. Meeting with the realtor, a friend of my retired uncle Phil who worked in real estate in the area for thirty years, to appraise the house and begin advertising it for sale. Taking Mom to the hospital to explain what's happened to the doctors and nurses she worked with for years. Making a last dinner for my uncle and cousins, Mom coaching me on how to use the pressure cooker (which still seems dangerous to me) and make gravy, since we're trying to keep Dad from doing his usual cooking work. Explaining to everyone what's happened and watching their faces and voices change. Pulling up roots, swallowing tears, keeping on schedule to finish what needs to be done.

Never be the middle man between two exhausted older people who are both hard of hearing and stressed out from making sudden decisions about how to dispose of things they've spent their life together building. Relatives and old friends have called and stopped by, and I've learned more than I was prepared for about sibling relationships and old conflicts. It's the last night in the old home and we've been through tears and rage and bewildering battles about issues I'd never known existed.

"Hello. This is Marie, Harold's sister. Who am I speaking to?"

"Hi, Aunt Marie. This is David. We're just finishing up here in Rupert, and we're heading back to Billings tomorrow."

"Oh, David, I'm so sorry to hear about Harold. I'd like to speak to him if he's still up." Her voice has softened into an Irish lilt that sounds exactly like that of their mother, Grandma Frances, who passed away years ago.

"Well right now he's finishing frying some pork chops, but he'll be done in a minute."

Her voice turns sharp and shrill. "He shouldn't be doing work like that now. Let me speak to Thelma, please."

Dad spears sizzling pork chops onto a platter, while Mom splutters indignantly on the phone. "Well you know Harold, Marie. This is something he wanted to do, and I didn't want to fight him about it. I think he's just fine, thank you."

Then Dad is on the phone, assuring Aunt Marie that he's doing as well as can be expected under the circumstances, slipping into a voice I'd never imagined hearing from him, of a brother trying to console and calm an older sister. "Well, they say I've got six to twelve months, Marie. So we've got time to settle things up here and visit with everyone back in Billings. I still get around pretty good on this hip, but I just have to be a little careful with it."

"I'll never speak to her again, even if she is your sister," Mom declares as he hangs up the phone. I've never before seen her so flushed with anger and shame, defending herself from what she obviously considers to be an unexpected assault on her credentials as a nurturing wife and, perhaps even more excruciatingly, on her professional competence as an RN.

"Oh, Thelma, you know Marie is just upset at the news," Dad says, playing an uncharacteristic role of smoothing over rather than provoking an argument. "She'll have calmed down by the time we talk to her again and we'll have forgotten all about it."

Savoring my plate of pork chops, mashed potatoes and gravy, and Dad's canned home-grown green beans, I realize that I've become an often-forgotten spectator to dramas in which my parents and aunts and uncles have shed their familiar faces. Preparing for death has re-engaged them in old family stories, while I try to figure out my new roles as caretaker and ambassador between wounded parties.

Later Dad yells downstairs telling Mom to come to bed, since she's suddenly decided to sort through the closets and the file cabinet the night before we leave.

"I have to take it easy on this damn leg," Dad fumes. "But she's got to come to bed and get some rest. She's going to make herself sick working like that." He's frustrated that he can't do anything, worried about Mom's health, and, as always, exasperated that she's ignoring his rational advice.

"Come on, Mom," I plead later, down in the basement. "We don't have time to sort this all out now. The movers will box it up and you can sort it out in Billings."

"Well, I'm not going to leave my home without our good clothes," she mutters. "And God knows what will happen to this stuff between here and Billings." She's eighty-one and has been sick a lot over the past few years. She only has one good arm because she shattered her left one when she fell down the basement stairs of my brother's home taking care of his kids while he was in the hospital. But her right arm turns like a windmill and clothes fly into two piles, one for the movers and one for the car. So I try to calm down Dad upstairs and I take orders downstairs until Mom finally quits after midnight and we all collapse into bed.

"Liz, we're not going to make it, honey," I explain when I manage to sneak in some phone time. "They're both going to end up in the hospital before I get them back, and I'm going to end up in a sanitarium. Where are these sanitariums anyway? I don't even know where to go to commit myself."

"At least you're getting to spend some time with him," she observes wistfully. "Sounds like you're all doing fine, considering." She once told me that after her father suddenly died part of her that was Daddy's little girl seemed to die, too.

By the next night we're back in West Yellowstone. Mom has been miserable and sick in the back seat, Dad has gallantly resisted saying I told you so, and we're all reflective, worn out from the hellos and goodbyes and pressured decisions, contemplating the enormity of what's happened. But that night, at a cozy ground floor dining room occupied by just ourselves and the waitress, I realize that we're all actually in surprisingly good spirits.

"It's done." I raise my glass in a toast. "We did it. I guess you're Montanans again as of now." I never did completely understand why they retired in Idaho after a lifetime in Montana, but Uncle Phil and Aunt Roma's family was there, and they liked the relatively tropical climate, the sumptuous fruit trees, and flourishing garden.

"And it feels good," Mom says, as she and Dad raise their

glasses. And for that evening at least it is good, as good as it can be.

As I drive back down the Yellowstone valley the next day Dad begins talking about the war. I've heard some of the stories, but never like this. As he speaks I comprehend for the first time what the war meant to him and Mom, because he'd really never talked much about it. But I also begin to imagine the stories of so many others like them in their generation— survivors of tough times growing up during the Depression who'd moved from their ranches and farms and small towns to pursue their dreams, dreams that had been suddenly swept away in the global upheaval that took many of them to the far ends of the earth, then returned them home again to reconstruct their ruptured marriages and lives.

After I left that hospital in Dillon I'd saved some money, so I went back to Billings to go to college at Eastern, he says, picking up exactly where he'd left off five days earlier when we'd last traveled this road. *That was 1941, and that's when I first met your mom's sister Roma and her fiancé Phil Bare and her brother Terry and his fiancée Ruth. It was through them that I met your mother there at Terry and Phil's apartment.*

We'd go out when we could, which was about once every two weeks, because those nuns at St. Vincent's Hospital were godawful strict. But then Pearl Harbor came along, and I enlisted the next day in the navy and they shipped me to California for my basic training. Your Mom wrote and told me she had graduated from nursing school and had gotten her first job in Palo Alto. So I went up to visit and we decided to just go ahead and get married there in Menlo Park.

We even found a priest to marry us, but he had to get one of the janitors to stand in as the Best Man. Then they shipped us overseas ten days later. But we couldn't tell anyone, not even our wives. I finally was allowed to write a few weeks later from Hawaii but the military censored everything, so you couldn't give any news about where you were or what was happening.

Pearl Harbor was a mess when we got there, and the navy was mobilizing everything that could float to the South Pacific. So the next thing I knew I was out at sea as a medical orderly on our battleship, the uss North Carolina. *Back in basic training they originally scheduled me for a desk job, but I requested to go into battle, for some damn reason that makes less sense to me now than it did then.*

After months on that water we'd actually want some action, anything to break the monotony. But then during an attack we'd lie on the deck in an airtight room praying for it to end. Just lie there, waiting to be blown to bits, hours at a time. Hearing the announcements. "Torpedo from the northeast." Waiting for it to hit. The big guns going, enough to knock you over when they went off. Men going psycho— every possible way. One kid turned into a religious fanatic, started screaming about whether God would forgive him for stealing tires when he was a kid. It made everyone a little crazy.

I was in my medical lab when we took the torpedo right on my battle station. The power of the blast nearly knocked me out, and by the time I got there the battle station was gone, turned into a blasted hole flooding with water. When we limped back into port I got assigned the worst damn job I've ever had, going in to retrieve the corpses. We walked in stinking water into the wreckage, feeling the floor with a rod to make sure we didn't fall into a hole. The smell was so bad you'd have to stop to gag your guts out before going forward. Believe me, there's nothing that smells as bad as a putrid human body. Then when you'd find the corpses, the gas would squelch out of them when you touched them, the hair and skin would come off in your hands when you'd try to move them.

Boredom and terror. You'd think you'd go crazy from waiting for something to happen, but when the fighting started you'd give anything to get it to stop. I saw our aircraft carrier, the Wasp, *go down outside the window in my lab. You probably can't imagine what it's like to see a big ship go down at sea and wonder if you're next.*

Then we started picking up the wounded marines who'd survived the landings. I was running a crew of fifteen men doing our best to patch them up, and they'd break your heart. I'll never forget this one poor sonofabitch, shot in the chest, missing most of his lung under the scars from his first two landings. "You know, Doc," he'd whisper to me. "I don't really care if I survive because they'll just send me back again. The first time they send you in because you're a rookie recruit. Then they send you back because you've got experience." A damaged man, a deeply damaged man. They were all shot in the chest.

So much of it was just luck. Some guys got stationed in Hawaii the whole war. Others had to make landing after landing until they were dead or as good as dead.

So I was one of the lucky ones who survived without any serious injuries, but God, something like that changes you. I guess a lot of us who came back were pretty different from the eager beavers we'd been when we first signed up.

When your mom and I finally got back together after the

war we almost didn't recognize each other at that bus station in San Francisco. I'd sent her a telegram telling her the hotel I was in, and she telegraphed back to tell me the bus she was coming in on all the way from Plentywood, where she'd gone back to work during the war. When at first I couldn't find her I thought maybe she'd changed her mind about the whole thing. And then we recognized each other and kind of reintroduced ourselves.

About nine months after that you were born up at the naval base there in Bremerton, Washington. I'd started working double shifts on a construction job, because building was booming there after the war, and I was so out of shape from those years in the navy I didn't know if I was going to make it. My hands were so blistered I could barely run those wheelbarrows of concrete up the ramps. But after a few weeks I toughened back up.

So when I finally got my release papers over in Seattle we headed back to Montana in that first old car we'd bought. And we had quite a trip, visiting friends and relatives, going back up to Plentywood, where I met your mom's family for the first time, then down to that Ashland country, where she met mine, all with a new baby. After that we got that first home with Roma and Phil up just north of here, while I started back to school in Bozeman.

By then we were approaching Laurel, just west of Billings, and I realized that our journey was ending. I stopped for gas at a truck stop and when I got back to the car after paying the bill Mom was worried because Dad hadn't returned, so I went to look for him. I spied him hurrying back from the far cash register. He'd just snuck away to buy the cigarettes he'd supposedly quit for years, and he was particularly careful to hide them from Mom now because after they diagnosed the cancer his smoking drove her crazy. He looked frail and already somewhat shrunken to me, limping back in his light jacket and his farmer's cap, but he also had the jaunty grin of a man who'd accomplished his mission.

Later, in alliance with the hospice supervisor, we talked Mom into accepting him smoking openly at home, since the damage was already done, and it was getting dangerous for him to sneak outside on his bad leg to smoke. And after that, when he was often disoriented and walking with an oxygen tube in his mouth, we kept his matches and cigarettes for him so that he wouldn't accidentally start a fire. He constructed some serious scenarios to try to get them back.

"I'll have you know this business about my missing cigarettes is under investigation," he announced sternly at one point. "I don't want to get anyone in trouble, but you'd all be better off if I just got them back." But by then he rarely knew who we were, and caring for him at home had become a series of anguished, poignant, sometimes even comic dramas in which he provided the cues to tell us the parts we played.

"I don't know who's in charge of this operation, but they sure as hell don't know what they're doing," he confided to me once, as I visited with him while Mom and Kirk and my sister Helen worked around the hospital bed that hospice had installed for him. I'd figured out that I was his confidante, and he was in some kind of dysfunctional retirement home, whose power structure he kept trying to pry from me.

Toward the end his dramas got increasingly bizarre. Whether his escalating disorientation was due primarily to the radiation treatments or the increasing doses of morphine or the effects of the cancer itself I was never quite sure.

"You know, I know where I am," he whispered to me once.

"I got captured on a mission somewhere here in the Middle East, but I don't speak the language and I'm not sure what I'm supposed to do next. I was hoping you could help me out." Sometimes we'd try to link him back to the reality we were all in, and sometimes we'd just play along to explore the strange stories he was living.

Some of the things he'd come up with were so funny and outrageous we'd crack up telling the stories, and others would leave us sad and contemplative for days. The odd thing was that he was so recognizably himself at the center of all the stories that wove around him. You could tell by his grin and style of talk what stage of his life he was living, as though his moorings in time and space had been cut loose, so that he could emerge as a cagy old veteran in a military hospital trying to figure out who the big boss was who knew where they'd put his cigarettes, or a young man involved in mystifying espionage operations for the military, or a wounded superintendent responding to a school board that has just voted to dismiss him.

"I understand the reasons for your decision, but I would like to make a closing statement."

I hear the deep seriousness in his voice as I come up the stairs late for breakfast. Everyone else, sitting in front of their bacon and eggs and hash browns, listens, stunned, as their food turns cold.

"I think he's talking to the school board in Ennis after they fired him," Kirk whispers as I slide into the chair next to him. Dad's in his wheelchair in the middle of the kitchen, searching to find the right words as he struggles with overpowering emotions.

"I'd just like to say that I've always tried to do what was

right for this community and these students." This is his formal speaking voice that we'd usually only heard at graduation ceremonies, only now there are no jokes to lighten his message. We feel him gathering his thoughts as he raises his head to look us in the eyes. Only he doesn't see us, he sees the school board assembled around him as he rounds off his statement with all the dignity he can muster.

"And I want to thank all of you who supported me while we built this new school and established some new programs." This is the pain he's always carried, I realize, this lifelong struggle to prove himself in some arena I'd never been fully able to visualize. "I wish you and the school well in years to come. I hope some of the things we've done we'll all look back on with pride. Thank you. That's all I have to say."

He slumps back into his wheelchair, obviously exhausted as he drifts off into another time and place. I pat him on the shoulder as I walk to the stove to fry bacon and eggs. I'm amazed that he can be so eloquent and precise in the middle of dementia. And I suddenly feel a connection to his story that goes beyond sorrow and analyzing where it came from.

He wants to end well, I realize. He shifts between memory and fantasy, but through it all he's mobilizing what resources he has left to end well.

The hush that has settled into the kitchen lingers for days.

By then it was spring of the following year, and we'd all lived through the changes in our various ways. We'd take shifts when we could get time off from our jobs to travel to Montana to help Mom and Kirk and his family, who, unlike the rest of us, lived with Dad's condition full time. Now he was dosed heavily with morphine to ease the pain. His skull was bare and burned from the radiation treatments that reduced some painful tumors but took such a severe toll that we were never sure whether they were worth it.

He was a small, wiry man to begin with, and now his body was wasted and frail, like that of a Holocaust survivor. But he never lost his earthy, cowboy sense of humor, never stopped trying to figure out what the hell was going on so he could get out of the fix he was in. And there were times too when we all felt closer to him than we'd ever been. After his ministroke following the radiation treatments, which left him disoriented with half his vision gone, Kirk and I philosophized with him in the living room one afternoon.

Events had shaken his tough cowboy pragmatism and his faith that reason and science provide the answers to all things worth knowing. "Christ, you just don't know what's real and what isn't sometimes," he confessed. "You think you've about got it figured out, and then something comes along that changes everything so much you realize you don't really know anything."

One afternoon shortly before he died, my brother Mike and I talked with him in the darkened room, each holding one of his hands from opposite sides of the bed. His body was wasted but his hands remained strong to the end, working man's hands still, though he hadn't done much hard labor in the last fifty years, except for the constant work in his garden and yard. But gentle hands now, gentle and calm.

My father wasn't exactly a holding-hands kind of guy through all the years I'd known him, and to tell the truth neither was I, so it was remarkable to me to take his hand so naturally during these hushed near-death conversations, when he struggled to figure out who we were and to communicate the strange revelations he was having. "Dad, this is David," I'd say, taking his hand, and sometimes he'd brighten with a broad smile. "Oh, David," he'd murmur, remembering who I was it seemed, deeply appreciative of the wonder of it all.

"Perhaps you guys can help me out," he asked us that afternoon, in a voice I'd hear sometimes from him and my aunts, with a lilt of the Irish that comes back in their stories about the old days. "I don't know where it's coming from. Maybe I heard it somewhere when I was a kid. But I keep thinking about this poem or song. I don't even know what it is or what it means, but it keeps going through my mind.

"No father's son
No mother's child
Known to none
Known only one."

He repeated the lines several times, wondrous that such words came to him now, searching to understand them. Later he told us with astonishment that he'd just realized he'd been wrong for a long time about something vitally important. "You know most of my life I've been thinking about this," he said. "And now I know I was wrong about the whole damn deal. I just want to say that I never ever meant anybody any harm, and I'm sorry if I ever hurt anybody anytime because I didn't understand." I never was certain whether he was talking about some misunderstanding that went back to his days on the ranch, or one of his old conflicts with Mom, or some of the strict discipline he'd doled out to us kids, or something cosmic between him and some larger mystery, or all of the above and more. Deathbed repentance and mystery and revelation, interwoven to the end.

Liz and I had just returned to Fort Collins in early June. The hospice nurse had told us there was no telling how long it would be so we might as well go home and rest for awhile. We'd been there two weeks, helping to change diapers and bedding during the last stages of his decline, which were actually much less demanding in terms of care. And the house was getting too crowded anyway, as the family began to gather to be with him at the end.

I had a few days to recuperate with Liz before my sister Helen called to tell me I should come back up. I left early that Thursday morning and arrived in Billings in late afternoon, riding once again that five-hundred-mile stretch of I-25 I'd come to know like the back of my hand. Everyone was there, even the grandkids. He'd been in a coma for two days, breathing in that barely perceptible way with the mouth open that I now know signals the last stages of dying. "Expiring," I thought. "Slowly, gently expiring." We were all there around the bedside at one in the morning when he expired his last breath and was still.

Strange that a difference that seems so subtle can be so profound, as though some deep music we could not hear but only feel had stopped, leaving hushed silence. The men in dark suits arrived an hour later, emerged from the room with the body, and wheeled it out the door. The room that had been the center of our dramas for so many months was empty. The next day the hospice volunteers came to say good bye and remove the hospital bed.

"You'll have to write the obituary now," Mom told me, taking me aside. I found the writing assignment strangely comforting during the next few days, while we made funeral arrangements and got out announcements through the *Billings Gazette* and by phone.

Dad had always hated seeing the body at funerals, saying that he'd rather remember people alive and healthy than to pretend that their corpses actually looked like them. But Mom decided to display his body before cremation anyway, for the sake of family and friends who had not seen him for so long. I was surprised to find myself comforted by the sight of him in the coffin, with such a look of repose.

During the service we "kids" sang some of the music he loved, and afterward I tried along with the rest of them to say something about memories of him we cherished. "He always said he was raised with two religions, Irish Catholicism and Ranching Republicanism, and he rebelled against them both," I said to the surprisingly large turnout of relatives and friends and even some of his ex-students from northeastern Montana who had settled in the Billings area. "But he was always proud of his heritage from this ranching country, and we all learned to respect and enjoy it through the stories we got through him and many of you."

Or something like that. By now I knew that the words we say at such times never quite express what we mean. So we all spoke and shared our stories and songs and buried his ashes in the plot next to what would be Mom's final resting place. And then we ate ham and scalloped potatoes and grouselot at the funeral dinner and left the next day from that old Yellowstone River country to return to our homes and lives.

"It's strange, Mom," I observe that next spring while we wait for our breakfast at J.B.'s, across the busy intersection from her apartment in Billings. "I've never dealt with anything as upsetting as Dad's dying, but sometimes I feel like I got closer to him and everyone in the family during all that pain and craziness then I ever did before."

She looks at me over her coffee with a thoughtful gaze. She's stronger and healthier than she's been in years. She insisted that I meet her at the restaurant rather than pick her up because she enjoys the walk, finding her way around the network of shopping malls that surround her new apartment complex. She loves the new furniture my sister Doris and I helped her pick out, and she says the layout in her apartment reminds her of their Idaho home. She loves reading and watching her Atlanta Braves (to whom she'd become devoted through watching cable television during their years in Idaho) and visiting with her children and grandchildren when they call or pass through, following no timetable but her own.

She sips her coffee and her voice softens. "In some ways he never really was the way he wanted to be except during that last nine months," she observes, repeating an observation she'd made to me the previous summer after his death. While he was suffering and dying, I think, trying again to comprehend what she means.

I'm still thinking about what Mom said the next morning, as I prepare to visit Dad's grave, then head west on my spring fly-fishing trip. Now my spring ritual begins with a trip to Billings rather than to Idaho, and I'm wondering what I'm really fishing for.

I travel these Montana roads after the long winter melts away, following fishing stories and memories, seeking connections. Sometimes they rise for dry flies, so that I can see what I'm fishing for and how to hook up. But usually I'm nymphing or drifting streamers below the surface, waiting for the sudden strike from depths I can't see that quickens my blood, a reward for my intuition or just a sign of good luck. Sometimes the fishing is even as good as I've been told, occasionally surprisingly better. I revisit cherished waters and discover new ones, listening to the old landscapes along the way, as I visit friends and family and exchange stories about what's happened since we last met.

Maybe I've really been fishing for these stories all along, I realize, looking to restore old connections and discover new ones. Though Dad is now gone, Mom and my brothers' families are still here in Billings, so the family at least temporarily is now centered back in this old Yellowstone River country.

And now I'm just beginning to see the shape of my own story. Perhaps this happens to all adult children when their first parent dies. As I look back on my life now I realize it's been a long process of leaving and finding homes, and that all along I've been closing a large circle to return to the home that I left as a young man. My new home is in Colorado, yet every spring I'm drawn back to these Montana roads and rivers, tracing out the origins of my own story, and of the stories my parents carried.

For years I've been gathering up extended family stories set in Montana that weave back for over a century, whose ending for our immediate family seems to have begun with Dad's death. Or perhaps the old stories will somehow renew themselves in this new era.

This is how it ends. This is how it begins.

While I search for the gravesite in the cemetery I'm still thinking about Dad's death, seeking to understand some mystery I can't articulate. And when I find it I can't resist a wry smile. The new military gravestone for veterans hasn't been installed yet, and looking at the inscription on the temporary plaque I realize that he must be grinning in spirit somewhere around me. "Harold Morgen," it reads. "1919–1998." It had always been one of his pet peeves.

"Christ," he used to say. "Everybody wants to put an 'r' or an 'a' into Mogen. The navy was the worst. I'd be in line to get my orders and some petty officer would yell out, 'Harold Morgen.' 'That's Mogen,' I would say. 'M-O-G-E-N.' 'There's no "r" in Morgen?' he'd ask, looking at me like I didn't know how to spell my own damn name."

But this time it took the new gravestone from the navy to get his name right in the end.

"Hey, Dad," I'm thinking. "It was a long road you traveled, but I'm glad you and Mom ended up back here in this Yellowstone River country where you two first met, where you always seemed at home." And then I ease my truck into the traffic going west on I-90, beginning to dream about the drive down the Yellowstone and the Gallatin to West Yellowstone, and fly-fishing the Madison and Henry's Lake, and all the stories I might encounter along the way.

Journeys East and West

Leaving Home

"New York City?" asked the store salesman, his eyebrows raised. We were in the finest department store in Williston, North Dakota, the largest city in the region, with a population of over ten thousand. But selecting college clothes for the East Coast was obviously not part of his routine.

"We're shopping for my son's wardrobe for college," Mom had said. "But we may need some assistance picking these things out. I'm not quite sure how to find what he needs for a big eastern school."

"Columbia University," I added. "Manhattan Island."

That's about all I knew about it, really. That and the fact that Columbia was in the Ivy League and the brochures that the university had sent me referred to the campus as "the Acropolis of Morningside Heights."

With that image in mind, I'd spent the summer trying to visualize my new home, what it would actually be like to live there. You have lots of time to think while summer-fallowing, riding a tractor pulling heavy equipment at six miles an hour for twelve-hour days, back and forth over mile-long section-length fields. I'd conjured up contradictory visions in the heat and dust of the long summer. I envisioned the glories of ancient Greece somehow reinvigorated and transported to the New World. A gleaming city on a hill, I sometimes imagined, with white buildings bathed in an aura of golden light.

The store clerk examined the brochure Mom had handed him, which itemized clothing recommended for Columbia men (it was still an all-men's college, another fact that I found inconceivable, since my only experience had been with small-town public schools). The brochure listed items such as a formal suit, a white bathrobe, and—most problematic, from our point of view, since we had never actually seen one—a tuxedo.

His eyes lit up. "I think I have just what we need," he proclaimed, to my mother's obvious relief, as he pushed to the corner of the room a ladder on wheels connected to a high shelf. I was impressed by the artful construction of the ladder. The store clerk rummaged through a dusty pile of catalogs, then descended triumphantly with the one he had been looking for.

"I thought I remembered getting this. It's geared specifically for fashions in the Ivy League."

I had just deposited my summer wages a few days earlier. Over five hundred dollars, representing eight dollars a day during spring and early summer for picking rock, summer-fallowing, and bucking hay, plus ten dollars a day during harvest, when you worked every hour possible for the month or so it took to get the crops in. Not much by the hour, but room and board in a bunkhouse was included, and since there really wasn't time or opportunity to spend anything except for gas and partying on Saturday nights, it was essentially all clear.

Looking at our shopping list I realized that most of my savings would go for these new college clothes, which might have bothered me more, except that it all seemed part of a ritual preparation for initiation into an inconceivable new life, in which these mysterious new garments would signal that I belonged.

New York City. Columbia University. Manhattan Island. Places that seemed as remote from the Montana Hi-Line as the worlds of Oz or Mars that I had grown up reading about. The biggest city I'd seen was Billings, and I'd only been there a few times. It seemed a bustling and confusing metropolis. In fact, what I considered my one significant city experience involved shopping in Billings for a record player.

After my third summer working on my uncle Phil and aunt Roma's homestead in the Snake River valley in Idaho, Dad drove down to visit and to bring me back to our home in Froid. My summers of irrigating and hoeing potato and beet fields always ended with my aunt and uncle explaining to my parents that they just couldn't afford to pay me yet. Since it was a family deal we had never negotiated a specific wage in any case, but they planned to make it up to me at some point in the future. But on this last summer they actually came up with a hundred dollars in cash as a down payment on whatever they figured they owed me. So at the age of fourteen I felt rich, and I told Dad that I knew exactly what I wanted, as we drove down the Yellowstone River valley to Billings.

My uncle Phil Bare aspired to be a gentleman farmer of the kind Thomas Jefferson envisioned. Though they were far from wealthy, he'd assembled an impressive small library through a mail-order book club he'd joined. I'd discovered a book about classical music in his shelves that summer, and had bought some albums based on its descriptions. The first was my prize, since it had Beethoven's Fifth Symphony on one side and Mozart's Symphony Number 41, the "Jupiter" Symphony, on the other—the two symphonies that I'd

determined from my reading were probably the most profound pieces of music ever written, by the world's greatest
composers.

I'd listen to them in the evenings after work with my eyes
closed, cranking up the volume on my older cousin Jackie's
nineteen-dollar record player, imagining the opening phrase
of Beethoven's Fifth as "fate knocking at the door," as the
book described it. And it turned out that Sophia, the Italian
wife of Uncle Phil's partner Fred, who lived across the irrigation ditch, knew and loved classical music. She was the only
other person I knew with a similar interest, and she eagerly
provided suggestions about which pieces to look for next.

"I think I like Beethoven the most," I reflected, munching
into a freshly baked cookie. It was a slow Sunday afternoon, a day off. I wasn't working on the ditch banks or in
the fields, so I'd wandered over to chat. After putting her
pot roast in the oven, Sophia settled in across from me at
the kitchen table.

"Beethoven's Violin Concerto, by Heifetz. Oh, you'll love
it," she sighed, sipping her coffee as she gazed out at the water flowing through the irrigation canal in front of the kitchen
window. She swept her dark hair back from her eyes, glowing at the thought of the soaring violin.

"Do you like Elvis?" I expected withering sarcasm, but
hoped for something more eloquent than the confused disdain he seemed to elicit in most grown-ups.

"Well, some of those songs are pretty silly." She refilled
her coffee cup reflectively. "But just the other day I heard that
new song of his, 'Love Me Tender.' It's actually the tune of
one of my favorite old Italian songs. I could do without the
heavy breathing, but he has a gorgeous voice."

I savored another cookie and watched the water run, contemplating the fact that it was possible to like both Beethoven and Elvis. Talking about music with her enchanted me as much as listening to a new record album.

I had acquired a small but distinguished collection of classical albums with the spending money my uncle and aunt gave me when we went to town, and my dream, I explained to Dad, was to buy a record player that would allow me to hear them the way I imagined them.

The product of vigilant Depression-era conditioning, with a family of six to support on his teacher's salary, Dad was usually in a hurry to get home and unalterably opposed to spending money unnecessarily. And he obviously was aware that I had an inflated notion of what my summer wages could buy. But he became sufficiently caught up in my enthusiasm to spend an extra day in Billings driving back and forth between every store in the city that sold quality record players, as I narrowed down my selection by playing the opening of Gershwin's *Rhapsody in Blue* on each of them to determine which had the best sound for the price. Again and again I'd listen to the wailing clarinet alternating with the full orchestra, savoring the precision and depth of sound on the new stereo systems.

Dad amazed me by paying the extra hundred-some dollars required to buy the Magnavox console, which quickly displaced the new television as the center of family entertainment. It also competed with the piano and the assortment of instruments—saxophone, French horn, clarinet, and trumpet—played by us four oldest kids, all members of the school band. In Froid television was still a barely functional oddity. We only got Channel 12 from Williston, with sporadically reliable reception, featuring NBC and a few local broadcasts like the *Fay Crush Talent Show*. Hosted by a farmer from Bainville, it starred among other regional talents our own Froid Trio, high school friends who modeled themselves on the Kingston Trio.

As Mom and the store salesman compared the Columbia brochure to the store catalog, I realized with apprehension and growing excitement that the departure I'd been imagining for the past six months was less than a week away. I'd get on the train in Williston and ride east for two days and nights across the country to Pennsylvania Station and my new home.

"Let's start with the suit," suggested the salesman. "Then we'll get shoes and shirts and ties and accessories. And we do have a white terrycloth bathrobe that's exactly what they describe. I'm not sure about the tuxedo, though. I wish I knew more specifically what they're wearing in Manhattan these days."

In the three-piece brown tweed suit I felt as I had on opening night playing my first lead role in high school theater, with friends and the faculty director fussing over my costume to prepare me to step out in front of the crowd, which consisted of pretty much the entire community. Only this time I had no idea what the script was, or who was in the audience—or even if a drama existed except within my own mind.

My upcoming journey had actually begun when a guidance counselor started visiting Froid once a month.

Dad had cooked up the idea, convincing the superintendents of three bordering schools—Culbertson, Medicine Lake, and Bainville—to pool their resources and hire a guidance

counselor to rotate among the schools. So starting my sophomore year William Rock was there every fourth week, ad-
ministering tests and calling us in for consultations. After
getting the results of a preliminary aptitude and intelligence
test he called each of us into his office for interviews. He advised some of us to take the ACT and PSAT tests the following year, and when he got the results he interviewed each
of us again.

"What schools did you send your scores to?" he asked.

The application form had asked for the names of three
universities, and I'd listed the obvious ones for kids who
were serious about college—Montana State at Bozeman,
and the U of M at Missoula—as well as the only other significant university that came to mind, Concordia College in
Minnesota. One winter our music teacher had taken us to
Plentywood to a Concordia band concert, when they toured
the Hi-Line.

"When you take the SAT, I'd like you to list these three
schools." He handed me a sheet with the names printed out:
Columbia University, the University of Chicago, and Reed
College in Portland. I didn't know anything about them, but
during my senior year, out of curiosity, I went in to his office to find out more, and eventually applied just to see what
would happen. When I received scholarship offers from the
University of Chicago and Columbia that made it possible
to go, my world changed.

Both sounded exotic and scary and exciting, but in the
end I figured that if I was going to leave everything I knew
to live in the fabled East, I might as well head for the heart
of Manhattan Island and the Ivy League. (In a reverse image of the famous *New Yorker* cover showing the world as
seen from Manhattan—a view that I came to share after liv-

ing there for eight years—my internal Montana map at the time jumbled Chicago and New York City together into a general notion of the "East" that started somewhere on the other side of North Dakota.) And after I accepted the offer from Columbia and received their brochures, the image of "the Acropolis of Morningside Heights" confirmed my sense that I was leaving home to enter the glamorous but ominous Heart of Civilization, where I could be transformed or destroyed, or perhaps just rendered invisible, by forces I could not yet fathom.

"Well, I think it looks just marvelous," observed Mom. She and the salesman and my sister Doris surveyed me as I inspected myself in the three-sided mirror, contemplating my image in triplicate in the heavy brown suit unlike any I had ever seen, with vest and matching tie and shoes.

"So this is what they wear?" I'd seen outfits like this in movies, but still found it hard to imagine dressing this way myself, though I'd mastered the salesman's instructions about how to tie the tie and display it properly within the vest.

"I believe it is," said the salesman with satisfaction, though we decided that I should wait until I got to Manhattan to select a tuxedo, since he wasn't certain about the style and would have to order it special delivery to get it before I left in any case. So I emerged with most of my wardrobe for Columbia and a couple of hundred dollars left over with which to buy my New York tuxedo.

The next time I put on the suit I was dressing in my dorm room in Furnald Hall for something called a "mixer." My roommate John, a fellow scholarship student from New Jersey who was wearing a simple sport coat, looked a bit surprised as I buttoned up the vest over the tie. I hoped he was impressed. As I walked into the student center a tall lean fellow in a blazer surveyed me and exclaimed loudly enough for me and his preppy friends to hear, "Oh, a tweed."

I stood there for several moments watching the other students file in. I had no idea what a "tweed" was, but I knew I wasn't whatever it meant. I saw lots of sport coats and blazers, and an occasional three-piece suit similar to mine, worn by men who seemed comfortable wearing them. I spun on the heels of my heavy brown shoes, walked back up to my room, and returned wearing my comfortable sport coat from high school. The three-piece tweed suit hung in my closet for the next four years, though I did eventually put it to use after I began teaching in public school.

In my white terrycloth bathrobe I felt ridiculously regal walking down the hall to the showers, but I continued to wear it anyway because I decided it looked good, even though at first it inspired curious looks from my friends. Most of them just threw a towel over their shoulders and walked the halls in underwear.

I have never had an occasion to wear a tuxedo, while at Columbia or since, and more than once that first year I reflected on my good fortune. Thank God that Williston department store didn't stock tuxedoes, I would think, contemplating the space next to my three-piece suit, where it would have hung as a taunting testimonial to my wasted summer wages.

At the freshman orientation we wore name tags that also listed our hometowns and schools. I had just introduced myself to one of the numerous graduates from Bronx Science High School.

"David Mogen. What a name. From Fwah, Montana. Wow, are you the only one here from Montana?"

"I think so," I replied. "But it's Freud, as in Sigmund. Not Fwah." I had recently realized the opportunities for humor provided by my hometown's name, and eagerly took advantage of my first opportunity to explore them.

He either winced or grinned, I wasn't sure which, a perfect response to my first Froidian pun. "But I'm sure you know that it's a French word that means 'cold.' 'Fwah'? French for 'cold'?"

Interesting, I thought. Dad had hired a foreign language teacher during my junior year, but he taught German and Norwegian, not French. As far as I knew no one in Froid knew that the town's name meant "cold" in French and should actually be pronounced "Fwah" instead of "Freud." Some French trappers had obviously frozen their butts there before the next generations of Northern European farmers arrived. But when I tried to explain all the complications of our town's name to people back in Froid, no one seemed particularly interested.

Manhattan was more amazing than anything I had conjured up during my summer-fallowing visions. After I checked in that first day at Furnald Hall—our room was comfortable but crowded, with just enough space for a bunk bed and two desks—I walked down to the lobby, eager to explore the campus and the city. I struck up a conversation with another student who had just checked in. He was an upperclassman who seemed to know the territory, so I asked for suggestions about what to do to celebrate my first night in New York City.

"If you'd just gotten off a train from the West, what would you want to see first?" I asked.

He reflected for a moment. "I'll tell you what. Let's go to Times Square."

I wasn't at all sure what Times Square was, though I'd heard the name. I followed as he led the way from the quad out to 116th Street and Broadway, then crossed to a kiosk in the center of the street. As he stepped up to the booth inside and handed a dollar to the attendant, I heard a loud roar emerging from beneath the concrete floor.

"It's here." He waved at me from the other side of the turnstile. "Hurry up."

I had no idea what was going on, but I handed the attendant a dollar and got five small brass tokens in exchange. I pushed on the turnstile. It didn't budge. My guide waved at me from the stairs to hurry, so I leaped over the turnstile. As we raced down the stairs I heard the attendant yelling as my new friend looked at me in astonishment.

"Why did you do that?" he asked, as the subway doors closed behind us.

"How do you get the turnstile to work?" I replied, realizing as I said it that there must have been a slot to drop the tokens in. By then we were hurtling under the streets of Manhattan in a train, and I realized that the term "subway" must refer to a literal underworld of such trains running beneath the city, a mirror image beneath the earth of the metropolis I'd spent the summer trying to visualize.

In Times Square I wandered entranced among the bright lights and huge buildings and traffic, before we stopped to get a sandwich and beer in a bar unlike any I'd ever seen, with its burnished wood and wall-length mirrors. I was pleasantly surprised to discover that in New York at the age of eighteen I was suddenly of legal drinking age.

"I'll take one, too," I said after my friend ordered a draft beer. I marveled at the bartender's technique, as he poured off foam from the frosty mugs and slid them down the counter to us. At home we glugged down cans of Great Falls Select and flipped them out the window to hear them clank into the ditch. At my friend's recommendation I tried my first pastrami on rye sandwich, savoring the new tastes along with the rich textures of dark wood and brass reflected in the mirror. I walked back onto the campus that evening filled with wonder, visualizing the skyscrapers and the neon, still vibrating with the roaring stops and starts of the subway.

"You should go downtown with Mogen," I overheard one of my new acquaintances say a few days later. "He stares at skyscrapers." He sounded friendly, but I suddenly felt conspicuous. It hadn't occurred to me until then that my eastern friends might be as amazed to encounter someone in awe of subways and skyscrapers as I was by everything in my new world.

After a few months I knew my way around the subways and the local bars and diverse restaurants, and I especially enjoyed exploring the possibilities of New York delis, with their fabulous array of sandwiches we'd take turns running out for when we were studying late. I'd used student discount tickets to hear the New York Philharmonic play classics that previously I'd only heard on my records. Initially I had no idea what to expect from the actual class work, but I soon discovered that everything came naturally once school began.

Those first years at Columbia still define my ideal of a liberal education, and perhaps it was all the better because for a country kid like me it was all so new and exciting. We read great books and discussed them in small classes. Everyone in the freshman class read the same texts at the same time in the core contemporary civilization and humanities classes, so discussion from the classroom would carry over into animated debate out in the quad with students from other sections of the same class. We wrote essay exams and papers about everything. I worked as hard as I ever had hoeing beets or picking rock, but at last I was doing full time what I'd dreamed of while reading late at night in bunkhouses, reluctantly turning off the lights to avoid falling asleep on the tractor the next day. To my surprise I made Dean's List the first semester, and finally knew for certain that I belonged.

During my junior and senior years I observed some of my classmates burn out and fail, though they had excelled at highly competitive schools like Andover, Exeter, Bronx Science, and Music and Arts—schools whose reputations I had gotten to know. I sometimes wondered if my small town public school background provided opportunities that were difficult to parallel in sophisticated urban and private schools, with all of their obvious advantages.

I realized by now that many of my eastern friends had been under intense pressure to succeed academically since they were young children. But I'd never really felt pressure about grades, and unlike most of my new friends I had no idea while I took the SAT exam that my performance could alter my life. I was actually hung over and had stayed up too late the night before, regarding the test as just another interesting challenge of no particular significance.

High school was a blur of activity, starting with band

47

practice before school and ending with football or basketball practice that lasted until supper. In addition to classes, sports, and chorus, there were class projects and school dramas, and we still found time for cruising in cars, and (after the sports seasons ended) drinking too much.

Small-town public schools not only provided opportunities to participate but a social obligation to perform for a passionate community. If you were at all athletic, the town depended on you to represent it on court and field. So students who would never have had the chance to compete in a larger school system learned the excitement and pressure of making plays against our Hi-Line rivals, when the outcome of a game could elate or devastate everyone in the community for months to come. And if you had diverse talents, they were all in demand. Until we became starters, several of us on the basketball team would do double duty. We'd leave the locker room to play with the band at halftime, since the band leader insisted that he needed us more than we subs needed to hear the coach's locker room exhortations.

And in many ways, from my point of view, the educational preparation in the better country schools like ours was sufficient and even liberating. We had excellent, enthusiastic young teachers in math and science, which were my favorite subjects then, and as I look back the relative lack of direction in literature and cultural studies actually provided a kind of freedom. I simply continued my childhood habit of roaming the library, reading whatever captured my interest. That included a Great Book series that the school library had recently purchased, in which I explored a collection of Platonic dialogues. I stumbled upon an old anthology of Renaissance drama, which led me to an anthology of Shakespeare. I read *War and Peace* because it seemed to be the longest novel ever written, which led to *Crime and Punishment* and a general fascination with Russian novels.

In a bunkhouse I came across a paperback anthology of plays by George Bernard Shaw, improbably stacked in with the romances and Westerns and random selection of best-selling fiction—which I also read with enthusiasm—so I'd be jumping up and down on the tractor to stay awake after reading until two in the morning to finish *Man and Superman.*

And there were a lot of bright, creative kids in our little country school. Most memorable to me was Mitch Malone, famed among the area kids because he looked so much older than his age that he could buy liquor if we drove far enough from home. He was the lead singer of the Froid Trio, and he somehow ended up owning not one but two 1949 Packards—one black and one yellow—which became two of the most popular party cars in the area.

But in addition to being a local character, Malone was a kind of resident genius. Living on their farm out on the Fort Peck reservation he'd developed a passion for philosophy after reading Bertrand Russell's *History of Philosophy*, and had accumulated a small library of books by his favorites, including Kant and Spinoza. He owned a collection of chess books and we all discovered that he had mastered a variety of openings after he organized the high school Chess Club, and then talked the science teacher into starting the Philosophy Club. Neither club lasted long, but they were entirely spontaneous while they did, and at least temporarily, they got us interacting about something other than sports, dating, and drinking.

By the time I had graduated from Columbia and spent a year in graduate school and three years teaching, I had become so at home in Manhattan that I'd actually started to view everything beyond the reach of the New York subway system, except for my home state, as distant provinces. In conversation with some teaching friends I made reference to the differences between the Montana country schools where I'd grown up and the crowded and chaotic Brooklyn school where we all worked, at I.S. 55 in Ocean-Hill Brownsville. A woman friend looked at me in surprise.

"You grew up in Montana? I didn't think there were any Jews in Montana." I realized that while growing up on the Hi-Line I'd never really thought about my ethnic identity this way.

"Well, I can't think of any I knew there."

"You're not Jewish?"

"Actually, my name's Norwegian. But I'm more Irish than anything else, I guess."

It had taken me a couple of years to understand why my name was so hilarious in New York.

The first time I wrote a personal check the store attendant looked up at me with suspicion. "Your name is David Mogen? Can I see an ID?"

After examining my Montana driver's license he exploded in laughter, waving my check as he shouted to his partner in the back. "Joe, come look at this. His name is David Mogen. Mogen David. David Mogen."

I knew that my name was also the name of a wine. As a matter of fact, it was the only wine I was familiar with back in Montana, since some families there would pull out a bottle of Mogen David Concord Grape on holidays to mix with grape juice or soda for a kids' treat. But that didn't seem to explain the level of response my name sometimes elicited in New York.

Finally a Jewish friend of mine realized I wasn't getting it. He explained some of the meanings attached to the phrase "Mogen David" and its connection to the Star of David, the significance of its being a kosher wine. I suddenly had the feeling that introducing myself as David Mogen in Manhattan was like a non-Christian in Montana introducing himself as Jesus Christ, without any idea why people found his name remarkable.

When I moved off campus after graduation and had a phone listed under my own name I was the only Mogen in the Manhattan directory, and I'd get phone calls about products. I got used to the refrain.

"Hello, is this Mogen David?"

"No, this is David Mogen."

I once received a two-page letter threatening to report me to the Food and Drug Administration, complaining about a twelve-foot piece of twine coiled inside a Mogen David sausage. "P.S. And you call yourself kosher!" the writer concluded.

My friend's explanation not only explained the impact of my name in my new home. In a flash it also revealed to me the general concept of urban identity and ethnicity. I began to piece together the intricate program everyone in Manhattan seemed to acquire without even noticing it, deciphering the meanings of last names and neighborhoods and speech patterns to "place" each other when they met.

After eight years in the city I was heading back west. I'd accepted an editorial fellowship in the graduate program in

English at the University of Colorado in Boulder for the following year, and though I'd loved most of my time in Manhattan, I was thrilled at the prospect of moving to the Rocky Mountains. Ever since I'd accepted the offer I'd felt growing anticipation and excitement, like Dad's descriptions of a horse heading home after a long day on the trail.

"Wow," my teaching friend observed. "I just assumed all this time that you were a New York Jew like most of the rest of us." Which I took as a compliment in a way, but a reminder as well of how much I had changed from the kid I was when I first arrived in Pennsylvania Station eight years earlier. Leaving for a new home in the West left me reflecting back on my first encounter with the East, when the dreams with which I'd arrived seemed so vast and inarticulate.

Back in that fall of 1963 I had waved goodbye to my family as the train pulled east out of Williston, and had spent the next day and night watching the Great Plains roll by, then Chicago and the Midwest and Philadelphia, before the final stretch through New Jersey to Manhattan. I had met kids from around the country who were traveling to different schools, soaking up everything I could while talking to them to prepare for life in a big city.

A tall redheaded guy from Seattle who was returning to Columbia arranged with me outside Pennsylvania Station to share a cab to campus. He probably watched with amusement as I craned my head out the window to see the skyscrapers and traffic. It was a bright afternoon, and to me that first ride up Broadway was a wild carnival of sights and sounds I tried to correlate with what I'd imagined.

There are frozen moments in my life that I remember as vivid, resonant images. One occurred later that fall, when I stepped out of Hamilton Hall after class to notice the strange hush that had settled across campus, as everyone converged into enlarging groups. At the center of each was someone with a pocket radio—hot new items back then—broadcasting the news from Dallas that John Kennedy had just been shot. I've tried to explain to my own students over the years the impact that moment had on so many of our generation, and perhaps after 9/11 there's something they've experienced to compare it to.

My own reaction was intensified because a month earlier I'd marched with the band in front of JFK at the Columbia-Harvard football game in Boston, which was interrupted just before halftime to announce the surprise arrival of the president and his entourage. We were especially thrilled as we prepared for halftime because our skit was an election spoof about "Barry Silverwater," which we had performed earlier in the Yale Bowl, only to have the sound system mysteriously fail until the Yale band took the field. So because no one had heard the skit anyway, we'd decided to do it in Harvard. And then JFK was there, and I was sure I'd seen him out of the corner of my eye laughing appreciatively as I marched by his seat at midfield, blasting away on my baritone horn.

The shock of Kennedy's assassination seemed to reverberate through everyone there on campus that day, and in retrospect it seems to me that that moment, when I looked out to survey the somber gatherings around campus in the eerie silence, marked the ending of an era that we all grew up in called the fifties. In that moment we felt the world begin to change, the first rumble of the political and cultural eruptions that would sweep us all into the sixties.

But that was a national moment of tragic premonition.

My own personal drama of transformation began that afternoon of my first arrival, at a point of stillness poised between the past and the future. I collected my bags from the cabbie at 116th Street and Amsterdam Avenue, split the tip and fare with my urban guide from Seattle, and marched with suitcases in hand into the center of the quadrangle of Columbia University. I walked up the steps of Low Library and turned to face the opposite end of campus.

Butler Library looked like a massive reconstruction of the Parthenon, and as I stood there on the steps leading up to the Low Library rotunda, transfixed, I read the names of the classical masters across the front. I could feel the presence of the statue of Athena towering above me. Frozen in wonder, suitcases still in hand, I knew that I had arrived. My summer-fallowing days already seemed far away, but the hazy visions I had constructed in those dusty fields were becoming real.

Honyocker Dreams

I had traveled east, to the heart of the Old World, to discover a new path back home.

I surveyed my Eastern European audience before launching into my introductory story:

"Geez, Dad. I wish we could live in the West." I looked up from my Roy Rogers comic book as he entered the room.

"You goofy kid," he snorted, surprised and amused. "Where the hell do you think we are?"

Where we were was 1953 in the Montana Hi-Line in Whitewater, population approximately seventy-five, just south of the Canadian border, thirty-five miles of gravel roads north of Highway 2. We had moved there a year earlier from the Rocky Boys Reservation.

Back then Whitewater was just home, the way the world was. And it hadn't occurred to me until that moment that the place where we lived had any connection to the romantic West I loved in books and comics and the few movies I'd seen.

I first told the story publicly in 1995 in Turin, Poland, in a banquet hall in a thirteenth-century gothic building at the Nicolas Copernicus Institute. I stood at a podium beneath a twenty-foot-tall portrait of Nicolas himself, beginning a keynote address for a Fulbright Conference about the cultural impact of the American frontier.

Still recuperating from jet lag, I had stumbled into the story the evening before, talking to James, the American embassy official who had arranged the conference. I was explaining the peculiar identity crisis that most "westerners" share, living in a place saturated with mythic images that refract the reality they know in bizarre ways, like crazy mirrors where romantic and distorted mirages of the past loom around mundane realities of the present. "Tell the story," he said. "It's perfect."

Arrayed in a great rectangle in front of me the next morning faculty and students sat in tall straight-backed chairs, like those in movies in which kings address their nobles, as I explained how Dad and a Roy Rogers comic first made me wonder about where the West really is.

"Where is the West?" I have asked my students over the years. "What's western? What's more western, Los Angeles or Cheyenne, Wyoming?" And then we discuss what we all sort of know. That the American West evolved as symbolically defined territory whose location and meanings have transformed in time and space. That today it remains an ambiguously defined region including most of the territory between the Mississippi and the urbanized West Coast. That it's also a set of archetypal images attached to the concept of the "frontier," historically the European-American free-ranging story for defining everything quintessentially American, perceived from an implied point of view from the East. All of which is constantly being reinterpreted to accommodate the complex intersections of multicultural points of view that represent our rich but often bewildering heritage.

Explaining where the West was and is and what it means was even more complicated in Eastern Europe and Russia.

After my initial lecture I spent a week in Poland and another in Belarus, Russia traveling to universities, lecturing and teaching about the American frontier. Many of my Polish and Russian students spoke excellent English, and they seemed enamored with certain romantic images of the West, especially of Indians. They were intrigued by but appropriately skeptical about the reality of the "American Dream" that flows from this legendary heritage of free land and opportunity for those equipped to claim it.

As I wove through the frontier symbolism in Hawthorne, Melville, Cather, and cyberpunk science fiction, I wondered if Copernicus, whose birthplace I had visited the day before in a medieval apartment a few blocks away, was listening. Perhaps he was brooding about how a simple direction had somehow become the creative and destructive cultural center of the last global empire of the twentieth-century.

So no wonder that, as an eight-year-old kid, I didn't recognize the connections between the small western town where I lived and the world of Roy Rogers. Figuring out where the West is was considerably more difficult than it sounded. There must be a comic book West, I concluded, that has nothing to do with where we live. Perhaps we're no closer to Roy Roger's West than to Tarzan's jungle or Ray Bradbury's Mars.

But it wasn't that simple either.

As I grew up I encountered more complex images of the West that seemed closer to reality, closer to home. Books like *The Virginian* and *My Antonia* and *The Big Sky* depict a wild and romantic past, but also the gritty homespun detail and laconic humor of my parents and grandparents and their friends when they reminisced about the old days.

That was the big revelation, which had never fully registered when I was young. My parents had been there. They were shaped by growing up during the final era of the Montana frontier. They disguised themselves as ordinary small-town fifties parents, but if I paid attention I could catch glimpses of their true identities. My father was a teacher and a school administrator, but he had grown up as a cowboy. My mother was a nurse and housewife, but she had grown up as a homesteader. I never really discovered a meaningful connection to Roy Rogers, but through my parents I felt connected to something real even in Laura Ingalls Wilder's sentimental reminiscences about little homes on the prairie and Zane Grey's cowboy romances.

So I have come to realize that like most westerners—perhaps like most Americans, since in some form most of us share this general frontier heritage—I live in a multi-dimensional West. It extends in time into a much-mythologized and only partially recoverable past, and in space into an intricate web of public and private places that connect past, present, and future. Like, for example, the Little Bighorn battlefield, where my family's old ranching country borders a contested public ceremonial space that defines competing versions of our transforming national identity. Or family places like the small graveyards outside of Ashland and St. Labre Mission, where my father's ranching ancestors are buried. Or the old homesteads in dry-land farming country north of Plentywood, where my mother grew up, which I remember visiting as a child before I had any idea what they would come to mean to me. Or the new gravesites in Billings, where I return to remember my parents by the Yellowstone River, where they first met and courted, back before the great world war transformed their lives.

So that is the cosmic map of the West, I have come to

across this earliest and most famous cowboy romance, but now I remembered that it was one of the few Western novels that Dad and Grandpa Slim referred to with respect.

Before Dad died he gave me Grandpa Slim's weathered old copy of *The Virginian*, inscribed with his signature. "S. E. Mogen," it reads, followed by an oval with six lines protruding from it and the word "Ranch, 1911."

"What's the design?" I asked Dad.

"That's the brand for the Bug Ranch, the outfit he worked for when he first came to Montana. He must have gotten this copy back when he was a young hand living in the bunkhouse. I'd forgotten I had this old book, but remembered it after you wrote that first essay of yours about *The Virginian*. I thought you might want it to help remember your granddad."

After finally reading the novel I recognized for the first time a powerful connection between the Montana world I'd left behind and the great American books I'd studied at Columbia and in graduate school. Though the Virginian himself was co-opted by the East in the end, I could see in the novel's cowboy heroes both my grandfather Slim Mogen and my great-grandfather Lee Tucker from an earlier generation who trailed the first herds into southeastern Montana. Later, when I read Willa Cather's *My Antonia*, I could visualize the female homesteaders as my grandmother Lena Wilson and my great-grandmother "Grossmutter" Heisler, transported from the Nebraska frontier to the Montana Hi-Line a generation later.

In my imagination the pantheon of names on Butler Library that transfixed me when I first arrived at Columbia sud-

think—a multi-dimensional space-time network that weav
together private and public space, that weaves history in
an ongoing process of self-discovery, filled with mysteric
black holes and wormholes and unexplored new worlds a
infinite lost connections. Perhaps Copernicus was actu
humming with delight to hear about the vast, mysteri
paradoxical universe that opened up after he shattered
old human-centered cosmos and the divine harmony o
spheres. Perhaps he realized that he himself was a cc
pioneer.

But even as I came to terms with my admittedly
ended and indeterminate cosmic map of the West, I re
that I confronted a more local problem. Within the c
of the West itself I traced the outlines of a more spec
lactic territory called "Montana." Through some r
ous process, especially in the thirty years since I had
away, my home state had become identified as the
West, "the last best place," a cherished refuge of wr
movie stars and celebrities and the Unabomber and
men—all acting out their romantic frontier fanta;
cape and new beginnings.

After my father's death I realized that I had beer
home both physically and intellectually ever sinc
mer of 1971 when I left Manhattan for the Ro
tains. During my first term in graduate school at
sity of Colorado in Boulder my American literatu
James K. Folsom, who wrote one of the first se;
of the Western novel, assigned Owen Wister's 7
alongside the familiar American classics. I con
title on the course syllabus with surprise and
During all my years of voracious reading I ha

denly opened up to include names and stories from the West in which I'd grown up. My seminar paper, "Owen Wister's Cowboy Heroes," became my first published article, and ever since I've been tracing out connections between stories of the West and the contradictory images of the American Dream. I became a specialist in literature and mythology of the frontier, embarking on a journey which had ultimately brought me as a lecturer to Eastern Europe, and was now bringing me back home.

Telling a simple story to introduce my first lecture to an international audience brought home a personal truth. At their deepest source, all of my theories explain to a young boy who yearns to live in the West that he's already there.

When I taught at Georgia State University in Atlanta during the 1970s people chuckled after I told them where I was from. A local DJ apparently had an ongoing routine about how Montana doesn't really exist, how there are signs that point the way but no real place there—a vein of humor I found at once both curious and disconcerting. But in the 1980s and 1990s Montana became chic, or at least notorious, and my mailbox at Colorado State became a depository for amused colleagues sharing the latest news from the cultural front: an essay review from the *Los Angeles Times* declaring Montana the new literary center of America, a cartoon depicting a Montana Chamber of Commerce map locating an array of sensationally individualist loonies within the established geography of legendary places, stories about Ted Turner and Jane Fonda's new buffalo herd, and the glut of celebrities buying up old ranches—all of which made determining my own location in this increasingly fashionable territory even more challenging.

As I began to trace my family connections to Montana I encountered a problem that I had never really noticed during my more cosmic explorations of the West. There were the expected discrepancies between image and reality, of course—like the fact that my father's cowboy name was "Poodle," a title that was apparently attached to his curly hair but hardly evoked the romantic aura I associated with Grandpa Slim, the tall, lanky cowboy who, I decided, could have been a model for the Virginian. Actually, his brother, my father's favorite uncle, looked the part the most—in the lone photograph that I remember he had movie star charisma, with his hat shoved back and a devil-may-care grin. But he went by the curiously Old World name of Ole, and obviously there was a darker side to his life that the picture didn't reveal. The other significant fact I knew about him was that he blew his brains out with a revolver one winter in a lonely line cabin. And there was the fact that the family ranch had been sold when I was small, because Dad had such bitter memories of the cattle starving and dying of thirst during the Depression that he decided to become a teacher instead of taking it over.

When I began searching for descriptions of my own Montana experiences within the existing Montana mythologies, I realized that the places where I'd lived were scarcely acknowledged on the current array of literary maps. Most of these maps display spectacular mountain and river territories of western Montana, filled with lore about mountain men, miners, and vigilantes, about corrupt frontier politics and legendary Indian nations like the Nez Perce and the Blackfeet—stories I absorb during summer travels, when fly-fishing rivers and visiting friends in Dillon and Helena and my Indian relatives in Browning.

Much of the rest of this literature maps the territory where my father was raised in south-central Montana: the Yellowstone River country of the Greasy Grass and the Little Bighorn Valley, where the mythic foundations for Frederick Jackson Turner's version of the American story were laid, where America's most romanticized tribes—the Lakota Sioux and the Northern Cheyenne—suffered defeat in the last great battles of the Indian Wars, and survived as conquered people in the new era of cowboys and homesteaders that included my ancestors from Ireland and Norway and Germany, all interwoven within two generations into some hybrid identity as frontier Americans.

But the places where my mother was raised and where I grew up in northeastern Montana—where were they on the cultural maps? Where were the Assiniboine tribes from Fort Peck Reservation, whose story seemed lost among the epic stories of the Blackfeet and Sioux and Cheyenne and Crow? Where were the farming towns sprinkled across the eastern Montana Hi-Line, built around grain elevators and bars? Where were the strip-farmed fields where we picked rock in the spring and rode tractors all summer in the ragged hills and wind? As Montanans we inherited powerful legends from ranching country and the mountains, but images of the high plains farming communities all seemed imported from the Dakotas and Nebraska and Oklahoma.

About the time I noticed the absence of these legends, the maps started to arrive in new fiction and memoirs. The titles evoke the missing landscapes, the stories only beginning to be told, the rediscovered territories where I search for old trails and abandoned homes.

Now there is Ivan Doig's novel, *Bucking the Sun*, which

chronicles the construction of Fort Peck Dam in the 1930s like an epic saga, capturing the drama of my parents' generation, fresh off the farms and ranches that failed in the Depression, united for a living wage in a vast transformation of the land they could hardly comprehend. And the most fascinating and curious revelation to me is not the story of the dam itself, but of the "Red Corner" up around Plentywood, my mother's hometown, thirty-five miles north of Froid where I went to high school. Notorious at the time for being "red," as Doig presents it, Plentywood actually elected a Communist sheriff and town government in the 1930s.

"I kept our family from joining the Communist Party," my mother confided in a hushed voice, as though someone might hear. "They threw the big parties we'd walk miles to get to and they had a big register for everyone to sign. But I never felt quite right about it, so I told them not to sign it." All of which seemed inconsistent with the northeastern Montana I knew in the fifties and sixties, where Communism was a sinister foreign menace for which I couldn't imagine any of my relatively prosperous farming relatives having sympathies. Places on the map not just lost but vigilantly erased, now coming back into view.

Now, too, there are Larry Watson's stories set in Bent Rock, a fictional northeastern Montana town closely resembling Plentywood. *Montana 1948* newly introduced the Montana Hi-Line to a national audience. And, more recently, *White Crosses* captures the perplexed identity of the region most tellingly through the confused consciousness of Sheriff Jack Nevelsen, a Montana sheriff who adheres to a dimly conceived heroic code as he strives to save his town yet doesn't carry a gun.

"See the white crosses," Dad would observe, as we gazed at the small markers in the ditch gliding by our car windows on our Sunday trips to visit Mom's relatives in Plentywood. We knew that each of them represented somebody dead from an auto accident. What stories were there, of recklessness in a country without speed limits, of teenage bravado, of the scourge of alcoholism so culturally sanctioned it could hardly be recognized? These emblems of tragedy were inseparable from the lifestyle and the brutal weather, vaguely spiritual memorials to our lives spent traversing windy spaces.

More recently, there is Judy Blunt's riveting memoir, *Breaking Clean*, about growing up female in the old ranching culture in the Missouri-breaks country south of Malta, an area that remained entirely unknown to me even during the years when we lived nearby. When I was a boy we lived in Canadian border country just north of there, in Whitewater, and never had reason to venture south of Highway 2 into the rough territory down by the river. Blunt writes from inside a culture I rarely experienced directly, but I suspect my parents never entirely resolved their own conflicts about the rigid gender roles she describes. She brings to life the ferocity of the winters, the battles across icy and muddy roads, the cultural isolation and beauty of growing up in open, rugged country where life still resembled an earlier frontier era.

And most fundamental of all in reconstructing my own understanding of eastern Montana heritage is *Bad Lands*, by Jonathan Raban, an Englishman's passionate reconstruction of the dreams that lured that first generation of "hon-yockers" from far-flung outposts in Europe and the East to be dumped into their new Garden of Eden, assured by all the science and poetry that the railroads could muster that rain would follow their plows.

"Come on, you honyockers," Dad bellowed on summer mornings when Mom was working in the hospital, while he finished his master's degree in Missoula and temporarily became a student househusband. "If you don't get it while it's hot, I'll feed it to the hogs." All of which was nonsense since we had no hogs and didn't know what honyockers were—but rousing and memorable nonsense, nonetheless. We kids scrambled for hash browns and bacon and eggs, and labeled the first official family reunion some forty years later the "Han-yaker Reunion," creating our own spelling since we'd never seen the word in print.

After perusing Raban's beautifully sketched-in map, I realize that our instinct was right. "Honyocker" defines not only our heritage, but the contradictions it contains. It reflects ranchers' attitudes toward the hordes of foreign "clodhoppers" who spread across the plains after the Hi-Line land boom of 1910, disdain for a next wave of greenhorns by an earlier generation of immigrants only recently become self-styled "natives."

Yet I suspect that the term expresses as much humorous self-irony as true conflict. My father's Irish great-grandparents who took up ranching in the 1880s would likely recognize themselves as honyockers, as would my mother's grandparents who first broke up the sod after the turn of the century. And my father came to realize that the small ranchers and cowboys he grew up with had more in common with the honyockers he married into than with the big ranchers they idolized.

And so it seems all of my journeys converge in this word— my journeys in theory and memory and my ritual summer trips to Montana. "Honyocker." My trails intersect in this old nonsense word from my childhood. With all of its insulting overtones and inherent absurdity, the verbal map it provides evokes both a place and a story. Perhaps after all of these years of exploration, I can finally locate my West, at least, and find my way back home.

Honyocker dreams, I realize, we inherited honyocker dreams. The dreams of people who came from the far ends of the earth to encounter ample space but too little sustenance, who discovered that 640 acres and get-up-and-go could only sustain them from drought and locusts if they learned to hunker in and survive, to appreciate good luck when it came and hope for better when things went bad. They were the ones who endured when rhetoric about the Garden rang hollow, who adjusted their dreams to accommodate the harsh but invigorating realities of the northern high plains, where dry land crops struggle to survive in country more naturally suited to granite rock and sage.

Perhaps we finally are charting the mythological geography of this Honyocker West of the eastern Montana Hi-Line, where dreams were sometimes fulfilled or shattered, but most often were just endlessly displaced among fractured landscapes and the interminable wind.

Homing in on the Hi-Line

Finding Home

By the time I got to know my way around a new hometown, it was time to leave.

And where was "home"? While I was growing up we moved through a series of small towns along the Montana Hi-Line, the three-hundred-mile corridor stretching west from North Dakota to the Rockies, and north from the Missouri River to Canada. But we also lived in Bozeman and Missoula while Dad went to school, and since we visited relatives all across the state it sometimes seemed that all of Montana was home. For a while, Idaho was home, too. When I was twelve I began working as a farmhand for three summers in a row at my uncle Phil and aunt Roma's Idaho homestead, nearly a thousand miles from my Montana home.

I was actually born at the naval base in Bremerton, Washington, where Dad was stationed during the last year of the war. When I was nine months old my parents moved back to Montana. During my earliest childhood we lived in the strip-housing barracks in Bozeman that served as married student housing for the flood of new students starting college on the G.I. Bill. I remember the strip-housing in Missoula better, where we moved when Dad started his MA in education. From the time I could first walk I wandered down any path that presented itself—at least, in those earliest days, until someone found me in time for supper.

Perhaps the early traveling served me well. We grew up

as nomads, moving north and east along the Hi-Line as my father's teaching career took us from one small town to another, to the borders of Canada and North Dakota—through Box Elder, Whitewater, Frazer, and Froid (which I consider my hometown because I went to high school there).

As a teacher's family in farming communities we were, oddly, both foremost citizens and transient, rootless exotics. By the time we moved to Whitewater and I began the third grade I had become the oldest child (of four, five, and six children in years to come) of the new superintendent, a role which elicited occasional deference and erratic abuse, and which pressed me and my brother Phil into reluctant service as chief protectors of a proliferating band of younger brothers and sisters. The new kids on the block, the new family in town—always new beginnings, new challenges, new possibilities. For a kid, at least, always something to prove, lessons to learn.

Finding a new home was exciting and as easy as riding across the Hi-Line. But after you arrived there seemed to be no end to figuring out where you really were.

Strip-Housing Days

In my first memory I'm searching for wolves. The nice old lady had enticed me inside after she saw me strolling down the side of the highway. She gives me candy and tells me not to leave, because the wolves might get me. I look out the picture window at the afternoon sun on the fields and distant mountains. I'm eager to see wolves, but I never do, because my father arrives soon to take me home again.

I was always on the move. But for some reason that particular journey began the peculiarly selective process of memory: the taste of candy, the anticipation of seeing something exciting and dangerous through the window (I had no idea what a "wolf" was), the old lady's comforting presence.

This excursion into the countryside had taken me farther than usual. I usually got lost closer to home, in the converted military barracks that served as student housing in Bozeman. In my earliest memories, usually with my younger brother Phil trailing behind, I wandered.

As my exasperated mother recounted, once we got a lead she couldn't catch us, though I was just three and Phil was fourteen months younger. Pregnant with Doris, Mom strained to catch up with us as we toddled away in high gear. Frequently she found us from a police car, after calling for help when she had lost the trail. Riding home in a police car was the frosting on the cake of our adventure, no matter how much trouble it meant we were in.

The only people more impressive to my brother and me than cops were the garbage men, who leaped from trucks and rode off valiantly on their monstrous steeds. A few years later we used garbage can lids as shields in our spontaneous "gang" wars when we played at knight errantry, perhaps trying to live up to the romantic ideal created by observing garbage men in action.

Strip-housing childhood. After-the-war-years. G.I. Bill and Baby Boom time in college towns teeming with kids. Bozeman and then Missoula, where Dad took care of us and began studying for his MA while Mom worked full-time at the hospital.

Fabulous Missoula. The strip homes ran to the base of the mountain, which we periodically tried to climb. Once we almost got to the top. I decided to run downhill to see how fast I could go and discovered the terror of losing control. Against my will my steps got longer, as though I were wearing seven-league boots. I couldn't slow down, I was accelerating every second, my feet barely grazed the earth and couldn't keep up with my hurtling body. Finally I just held them together. Splat! My brother Phil observed that if I didn't have a nose I'd have broken my glasses.

We wandered by the stream that led out into the country, where I saw a boy not much older than I catch a small trout. When I was small I spent hours at a time fishing in mud puddles with cotton string and a safety pin tied to a stick. The instinct was there, but I'd never actually seen anyone catch a fish before.

We played at medieval warfare in the junkyard. Once we even scheduled a battle between opposing neighborhoods, armed with our garbage can shields and stick swords. But a crazy tough kid on the other side tied a piece of heavy metal on a rope and defended the high ground by whirling it around his head. Our war party decided to go read comic books.

Unlike the small towns Dad taught in, Missoula had movies. We saw Tarzan films, Disney's *Peter Pan*, *Davy Crockett*, and the unforgettable *River of No Return*.

Best of all was the Missoula A&W Root Beer stand. In my early twenties, just back from New York City, traveling with my first wife while trying to salvage our brief, doomed marriage, I pulled off the highway and searched until I found it—a nondescript drive-in next to a baseball stadium. We drank cold root beer as I tried to piece the memories together: the tray next to Dad's car window, filled with five-cent root beers with white foam boiling over the frosted mugs, amber light shattered through the glass—a thrill against which all other experience could be measured.

I went on quests for Aunt Imelda—Great-Aunt Imelda actually—who was married to my Blackfeet uncle Gene Ground, who, like Dad, was going to school on the G.I. Bill. Her baby had just been diagnosed with Down syndrome and she hoped to cure her at a mission in Canada. She would hand me a ten-dollar bill, as my bright-eyed little cousin Mary Ellen scampered in and out of the room. She dispatched me to the A&W to get not only root beer but cheeseburgers and fries as well. I was the queen's courtier conducting state business, solemn with responsibility. But the root beer at home, outside the frosted mugs, just wasn't the same.

Barefoot summers. I've lost my shoes again. We're going to a movie, so I have to find them. They're huddled in the back of the closet. Excruciating discomfort. They don't fit right anymore, they're lumpy and deformed, broken to the contours of feet that no longer exist. By now my soles are as tough as shoe leather, black and hard. I can sprint barefoot on asphalt, on gravel. Inside socks, cramped back into shoes, my feet throb, suffocating. They sweat. They itch.

Summer was short, too precious to waste. Heavy rubber boots brooded in the cellar, waiting for the interminable ferocious winters that dominated the year, that bundled us all into layers of clothing, and huddled me in front of heaters for years to come, endlessly reading with the hot air blasting on my spine. I still cannot imagine why anyone wants to ski. Summers are for running free (now I go fly-fishing when I can), winters for reading and work and hibernation. But my feet have been domesticated since those early years. Now, even in summers, they run in comfortable basketball shoes, their wild-animal, wandering days distant in the past.

Hudson Years on the Rocky Boys Reservation

Dad loved Hudsons and so did we kids. Both he and the superintendent drove one. There were Wasps and Hornets, and the Hudson Hornet was in a class that even we couldn't afford. Dad told us they could go one hundred miles an hour, which to me sounded as fabulous as magic carpets.

We lived in Box Elder on the Rocky Boys Reservation, where Dad began teaching and my brother and I finally started school. We were impatient to read. Parents then were pressured to slow their children down rather than speed them up. So we were each allowed to learn one word. We'd read books, looking for our word. Mine was "the," so I found it a lot. "The . . . the . . . the . . ." On to the next book.

Our Hudson was just the most obvious sign that we were rich. Actually, I don't remember the car so much as the sense of family pride evoked by the name. Riding back and forth from Havre—where everything important happened, where Mom and Dad would go to get the baby—we'd look for other Hudsons. They were few and far between. Most were Wasps like ours, but occasionally we'd actually see a Hornet.

We must have been rich. We lived in what seemed to me a mansion, an old farmhouse with a huge curved stairway going to the upstairs bedrooms. Designed for Christmas mornings. Sneaking down the great sweep of stairs before the folks were up, to the towering tree, feeling the gifts, trying to make out what they were under the dim Christmas tree lights. Huge cottonwoods and box elders shaded the yard, profuse with dandelions in summer. Vast spaces in which to roam.

I didn't realize that our local railroad was sinister and romantic until Dad's mom, Grandma Frances, came to visit while the baby was born. She told me that babies grew on cabbages, so whenever we'd go to the hospital—the most impressive place on earth—I'd look for the fields where little kids emerged from the tops of rows of cabbage stalks. Before my brother Mike was born I thought we'd all go pick out a baby together, make it more of a family affair. But the closer we got to the event the more it became none of our business.

Before we went to sleep Grandma Frances told us stories about horses and kids and bums. In her adventure stories we were the heroes. I had a palomino and Phil had a bay. Whatever happened it was exciting—like novels by Zane Grey, I would discover later. But the stories that fired my imagination most were the true ones. About the hoboes who would wander over from the railroad yards by my grandparents' home in Forsyth and do chores in exchange for a hot meal. For some reason this struck me as dangerous and exciting. Wandering strangers at the door. Hoboes. Bums.

We had a railroad crossing through Box Elder, too. And we had a large pantry area on the porch, with old cans of paint piled on shelves up by the ceiling. The connection between the railroad and the old paint cans didn't occur to me until after Grandma Frances was gone, leaving behind images of hoboes at the door. We had a new baby and Mom was trying to rest. "You know," I explained to Phil, "we've got to do something about the bums." He was only four, so sometimes he couldn't see the obvious. "We've got to paint the door shut so they can't get in."

So we solemnly went to work, climbing up the old stove to drag down paint cans. Glorious combinations of colors— green, red, yellow, black. We smeared them on the kitchen door and surrounding frame, inside and out, but somehow couldn't get the door painted shut.

"Boy," said Phil. "Mom's gonna like this."

"Maybe we'd better not tell her," I reflected, as she came through the door then hysterically phoned Dad to come home from school and clean up his sons' mess.

In Box Elder I first encountered death. We adopted a stray dog, a black and white mongrel that ran away. Then we got the puppy that got hit by a truck. We hadn't even agreed on his name yet. I lifted him carefully from the dust and cradled him in my arms, determined to make him better. The puppy still looked okay, but he didn't frisk around anymore, yapping and chasing after us. He lay by his food bowl and looked sad. We couldn't cheer him up.

When we came back from a weekend trip he was gone. Sitting on our bed before we went to sleep that night, Dad launched into a bedtime talk—an unprecedented ceremonial act, which alerted us to the importance of the event.

"The puppy died," he explained. "It will never return." The next-door neighbor had buried it while we were gone. Dad's words settled into me like the slow chill of the grave. Our neighbor had been just a big farmer with a truck, but now I regarded him with solemn awe, like a priest.

Ricky Johnson, an orphan, was the best player in our six-man football conference and a hero in Box Elder. I knew he was a hero when I saw him come off the field with bleeding cleat marks on his face. Face guards on helmets hadn't yet been invented, and an opposing player had stomped him. Oozing blood defined the cleat pattern as the coach tried to talk him into staying out, but he refused. He was in on the next series and bodies flew as he dragged three players down the field. The small crowd standing on the sidelines (we didn't have bleachers) shouted with excitement, while fans in their cars honked their horns. To see my hero afterward in the school halls wearing ordinary clothes was to realize that gods could disguise themselves as mortals and mingle on earth.

"He died in a freak accident," Dad explained, sitting on the bed again in what had become an ominous posture. He'd been out shooting with his friends. High school kids in Box Elder entertained themselves by mimicking movie shootouts, glancing bullets off boulders that their friends crouched behind, as well as by playing chicken in cars. But according to the high school kids my hero had never played these games. He threw his .22 pistol on his bed in the small local hotel where he lived. The bullet got him in the heart.

Death. The playful yapping puppy, his tiny tongue lolling out in excitement. My blood-stained hero in the hot sun and dust, racing back onto the field, invincible. Bodies in the cold earth. Exhausted with grief, I'd finally drift off after crying myself to sleep.

In Box Elder I first felt the pangs of young love. In the first grade I alternately adored Nancy and Janice, yearning for some consummation of romantic feeling all the more intense for having no definable goal. And later I became devoted to Tanya Stiffarm, an older sister of my Indian friend Danny, who lived down the alley—an unspoken attraction that was heightened after her father brought us buffalo steaks as a gift, food which only Indian people possessed, which tasted like beef but connected us somehow to exotic tradition.

We had the Hudson, we lived in a mansion for a year, and I thought we were rich. We posed for our only family photograph during our last year there—a family of six by then, with my new baby brother Mike—and looking at it forty years later I was startled to see how handsome and vibrant we all appeared. My parents look remarkably like a movie star couple from old black and white films. A black and white portrait, a formal 1950s pose, all smiling at the antics of the cameraman—the image of a family ideal that I hadn't realized we embodied so vividly.

I know now that my father began teaching at $3,600 a year, that we lived in a "mansion" only because the school couldn't provide reasonable housing that first year, and that he was borrowing money from his parents and frantic about how to pay the bills. It cost ninety dollars a month just for the coal to heat our fabulous home, and new babies kept arriving every year or so. Discoveries about life and death, unfolding mysteries. My parents knew better, but to me those were prosperous years, in that dusty little town on the Rocky Boys Reservation, when we were still enclosed in the Hudson's magic.

The Whitewater Time Warp

After Dad accepted his first job as a school superintendent we moved into a time warp near the Canadian border. I was eight when we pulled into Whitewater. Population seventy-five. Thirty-five miles north of Malta off old Highway 2. Paved road for ten miles, the rest gravel. Distance traveled not only in space but in time, back into a small-town frontier past. Antelope and jackrabbit country. V's of ducks and geese descending from the north. Tough dry land strip farming. Hills carved by glaciers in the Ice Age.

We kids decided Whitewater was all right when we eagerly walked downtown to turn in our harvest from highway ditches. Convincing Dad to participate in one of our favorite rituals on our way to our new home, we'd talked him into letting us off by the highway and driving a mile or so ahead to wait. We patrolled the ditches on either side, treasure hunters with eyes trained to scan for bottles thrown in the ditch—longneck beer bottles and soda bottles for which bars would pay deposit money that we could invest in candy, a rare treat. Many of the bottles were ancient and muddy, and occasionally we would find one with a drowned field mouse inside, but we proudly deposited our treasure in the trunk when we arrived back at the car, anticipating receiving change in return at the local bar.

To our delight we discovered that Blackie's Bar in Whitewater paid a nickel each for soda bottles, rather than the three cents each we had been used to in Box Elder. "This new town can't be too bad," I thought as we selected candy at the small grocery store on the opposite corner of the street. At least here they pay top money at the bar.

For a town so small Whitewater had a sizeable population of bizarre old bachelors. "White Bill" lived in a shack behind our home. His name was actually Bill White, but my little brother Mike—who became his buddy, lured by candy—got the names reversed and the reversal stuck because he was such a disheveled old coot. White Bill had a peculiar reaction to loud noises, reputedly some kind of a panic reflex from his experiences in the war, which made him the vehicle for local humor at Blackie's Bar. If someone spooked him by clapping their hands or yelling in his ear, he'd punch the first person he saw—usually the guy sitting on the barstool next to him.

This all came home when "Red" Ganley, the tall red-haired teacher who roomed in our basement, walked in after work one afternoon with a black eye. A few weeks later Dad, another victim of Bill's panic disorder, had one, too. Red had gotten his revenge. I couldn't figure out why anyone sat next to White Bill. Black-and-blue musical chairs. Half the men in the area had black eyes at any given time. The other half snickered with glee. But White Bill was merely eccentric compared to some of our more exotic bachelors.

Stinky was the most notorious, since he lived right there in the middle of town. We town kids—ranging in ages from six to eighteen—would be hanging out in the grocery store when a lookout by the window would yell, "Stinky!"

"Oh, geez, here he comes," someone else would shout, racing to the window for confirmation. We'd stampede out the back door before he arrived, leaving the hapless girl who worked there to her fate. So I never actually smelled him, though after our return we would all swear we were stifled by the lingering odor. But I did see his home. It looked like a large outhouse in a mud hole in the lot behind Blackie's Bar. Inside there was a filthy cot, a tiny blackbellied stove, and Stinky. A rumor circulated among the kids that he didn't take down his pants to go to the bathroom.

Most spectacular of all our renegade exotics were Bill Reitner and his sister Jane, who appeared periodically from wherever they lived out in the vast countryside. They arrived in style, by railroad, pumping an old hand-driven railroad cart they had somehow acquired. She was tall, rangy, weather-beaten, wild-eyed, dressed in motley and spectacular profusion compared to the modest fifties dress of the housewives in town. Perhaps my associations with exotic dress were enhanced by another rumor, communicated to me by my third-grade friend who whispered that she didn't wear underpants. He knew because his father was the local mechanic who scooted under cars in the garage, and thus had a privileged view, which apparently he had described to everyone in town.

But Bill Reitner was the local character in an area where, at that time, one might have been hard-pressed to find normal citizens by less provincial standards. He was huge—about six feet five inches and over three hundred pounds, with wild hair, a spectacular beard, and a massive belly. Even by Montana standards he was a prodigious, legendary drunk. I was once told he could talk when sober, but I never saw him sober, and in my own few encounters I remember him grunting and shuffling like a shambling grizzly bear.

I first encountered Bill in the café, across from Blackie's Bar (which was across from the garage, which was across from the grocery store—all four corners constituting downtown Whitewater). Reitner floundered in and the waitress quickly gathered up all the catsup, mustard, and Worcestershire bottles in sight, an activity that struck me as merely peculiar until after the next time he appeared at the café. The waitress was busy with customers and didn't see him come in. He slouched into a seat at the counter, opened a bottle of catsup, and guzzled it down straight from the bottle.

For years Blackie the bartender had tried to create something Reitner wouldn't drink, but he had never even gotten him to register surprise, though he used red pepper, mustard, Tabasco sauce—anything noxious that wasn't actually poison. Dad remembered seeing Reitner emerge from the grocery store with a jar of pickled pigs' feet, which he dropped and broke in the gravel street. He struggled to his knees as he shoveled pigs' feet with his huge hands into his maw. Dad swore he could hear gravel and glass crunching while he grunted and fed.

Bill Reitner's legend was constructed by such feats. In midwinter he crawled under the lumber piled in the lot behind Blackie's Bar. Early one particularly cold morning, when the temperature was around forty below zero (not terribly unusual along the Hi-Line) he knocked on the door of Blackie's home, not to seek shelter, but to thaw out the cans of beer that had frozen overnight in his overcoat pockets. In my imagination he seemed both subhuman and superhuman, a harmless but impressive mountain man relic from a wilderness past in which men could be unfathomable vehicles of appetite and energy. He spoke no human tongue, and he was indestructible.

Winter. Whitewater, first and last, was a small outpost of precarious heat and light designed to preserve us through the winter. The wind never stopped, which meant we lived from blizzard to blizzard, and the temperature often dropped to twenty below. (The record in the two years we were there was fifty-two degrees below zero.) The town had only been hooked up to electricity six years before we arrived, so everyone still relied on coal-burning stoves and kerosene lamps when the lines went down in bad storms. This disrupted my strategy for enduring the season, because the lamps provided a ghostly illumination sufficient to get around, but inadequate for reading in front of the heating vents.

How did people survive winter before electricity? I know now about the old tradition of telling winter's tales to lighten the long dark nights. But though we lived temporarily in a time warp we were essentially a modern family, without such traditions to sustain us. I waited for the electricity to return so I could sink once again into other worlds through books.

By now my brother Phil and I read avidly and my parents had long ago abandoned their earlier halfhearted attempt to supervise our reading habits. Once a month we'd get to Malta to visit the county library, from which we would emerge with boxes of books, sometimes over fifty at a time, a pattern that continued in libraries across the Montana Hi-Line throughout our childhood. Whenever we moved the first trip to the new library became an exciting scouting expedition in which we plotted out an exploration strategy for months ahead. Each foray yielded romances distributed among the vital areas—Western, science fiction, historical fiction, fantasy, sports—plus a miscellany of anything that caught our eye, from history to science to philosophy.

Certain series became favorites. I would eagerly scan the Edgar Rice Burroughs shelf hoping to find some of the rare science fiction romances along with new Tarzan adventures. I seem to be the only reader in history who admits to having had a passion for Freddy the Pig books, in which talking animals embark on grand quests, and I never have forgiven George Orwell for luring me into *Animal Farm* under false pretenses and turning my animal romances to horror so that I never could be entirely comfortable with Freddy the Pig again.

Most Montana libraries had decent collections of western writers such as Zane Grey, Max Brand, and Clarence E. Mumford that helped establish my fascination with a West that, like all my favorite romantic settings, seemed immensely far from home.

But the acid test of any new library was its collection of Oz books, for by then there were fifty or more titles by numerous authors in the series originally begun by L. Frank Baum, and our appetite for them was boundless. Each library had volumes others lacked, but they had to be savored a few at a time, so as not to use up a new supply in one reckless orgiastic month.

We browsed relentlessly in libraries, but I also discovered more exotic sources to feed my habit. Dad had boxes of old college texts, most of them unutterably boring, but among them I found a curious old green book called *The Divine Comedy*, the Modern Library translation, which I browsed in originally looking for humor. I couldn't find anything funny, but there was just enough lurid detail about torments to keep me turning pages, tantalized, for hours at a time.

From ages eight to ten I also developed a taste for men's magazines, which my parents accepted with remarkable equanimity now that I look back on it, though at that time the magazines that most interested me specialized more in adventure and hunting stories than in anything risqué. I couldn't figure out why they included irrelevant pictures of women in men's magazines. On our monthly trips to Malta Dad would give us each fifty cents or a dollar—a fortune—and I would sift through the magazine rack of the local drugstore, intent on finding the best value for my money, impatient with the owner's attempts to steer me to Little Golden Books, before finally settling on the issue of *For Men Only* that seemed to contain the most spectacular photos and hunting stories.

In Whitewater Dad was still a teacher. But now he was also the superintendent, which made him the boss of the other four teachers in the school system, one of whom taught grades one through four (the classroom containing my brother and me), another grades five through eight, and the other two—along with Dad—the high school. We had no real coach the first year, so Dad talked Mr. Gaunt, his new teacher from divinity school who had never played sports, into taking the job.

We cheered fervently for the Whitewater Penguins. "Fight, Penguins, Fight!" we chanted as yet another game slipped away to larger, more talented teams from Saco, Hinsdale, Dodson, Hoagland. We only had six players. The other high school male was crippled, so he served as the water boy. One of our stars played with black tape wrapped around the soles of his shoes.

The gym floor was so small that the free throw keys almost intersected, and in the rotten spots the ball didn't bounce correctly. This gave our Penguins a never-sufficient advantage over visiting teams, who never quite overcame their surprise at the dead spots. The crowd sat huddled on the small stage or strung out along the single line of folding chairs that barely fit between the out-of-bounds line and the wall.

The school buildings themselves were anachronisms. Two identical, institutional green buildings side by side on top of the hill, one the elementary school, the other the high school. Salamanders scuttled in the basement tunnel that connected them. Before his second year there Dad recruited a new coach—our relative Jimmy Corr, my new hero—who organized the high school boys into a work crew during study hall to tunnel under the gym floor in a futile attempt to fix the dead spots. With a real coach our basketball team actually won a few games that year and even—to the joyful astonishment of all Penguins fans—fought their way into the semi-finals at the district tournament.

We grade school kids trickled down during recess to observe progress on the tunnels and to catch salamanders. We usually killed them, but for some reason one dying salamander struck me as tragic, and my emotion struck a chord with the rest of the class. We organized a funeral in the schoolyard and I was just concluding a moving eulogy to bowed heads when Mrs. Brown called us in from recess.

Waiting for recess. Eight years of grade school, waiting for recess. It's now fashionable to long for the good old days when stern teachers taught the three *R*s, but I remember elementary school as a stifling bore. A prison. I couldn't read what I wanted, and school often kept me from reading at all. I would get punished for furtively reading under my desk, assigned an extra hundred subtraction problems to keep my mind forcibly focused on arithmetic.

Only during recess were we free. Recess was the thrill of escape from civilization. When the clock finally hit 10:30 we exploded into the outdoors, frantically playing, fighting, and flirting until the teacher appeared to cage us up again until noon. My new glasses enhanced this inconsistent reality—alternating between stifling confinement and explosive release—since now I often saw everything from a cockeyed perspective. My glasses were usually slantwise across my eyes, falling off my nose, and tied with string to replace a broken bow until the next time we'd get to Malta for repairs.

During our second year in Whitewater recess turned crazy for awhile. A local farming couple had finally succeeded in adopting a nine-year-old boy from the state orphanage. Even in that tough town and era, no one, including the horrified new parents, knew how to handle him. I listened as Dad talked with a neighbor about how the kid randomly destroyed things and—most unthinkable of all—vomited at will. He was a raving outlaw of my own age, a violator of all taboos who turned the school playground into a gothic horror movie set. He once found a dead animal, wrapped the rotting guts around a stick, and somehow used it to herd the howling girls into a nearby root cellar. Shrieking and gibbering in the light of the entranceway, he danced like a delirious ape as the girls wailed in terror in the darkness while he stabbed at them with the reeking flesh. We boys watched, too paralyzed to even think to intervene. Shortly afterward the boy disappeared. Recess returned to its normal level of explosive pandemonium.

When Dad told us we were moving to Frazer, two hundred miles east down the Hi-Line on the Fort Peck Indian Reservation, I cried. Our backyard went twenty miles in any direction, and when we escaped from school we kids roamed the hills and Whitewater Creek like wild animals. We hunted along the banks, rising over the creek below to flail stones at startled mudhens, ducks, even Canadian geese, as they boiled up from the water. Once, hunting alone, I surprised a great blue heron. Its massive wings beat up toward me as I valiantly held my ground on the bank to hurl my stones, then spent the next hour sitting in the long wild grass as it danced in the wind, absorbing the shock and thrill, watching the water flow.

Frazer was a small town on the Fort Peck Reservation, but to move there from Whitewater was to leave a wild and exotic past to enter the modern world. Mom didn't seem saddened at all by the news that we were moving. She seemed giddy with relief. But then she had never stalked wild birds along Whitewater Creek.

Two Worlds, Fort Peck Reservation

In Frazer two worlds traveled together, hardly intercepting each other's orbit. Over two hundred people lived there (it seemed a crowded city after Whitewater); half were white, and half were Indians. White people lived in the west side of town, in three or four blocks of white frame houses, and the Indian people lived to the east in log cabins. Although we all lived side by side, we inhabited different worlds and rarely crossed between them. We kids all went to school together, played, fought, then returned to our worlds separated by boundaries we couldn't have seen if we had tried. None of the white people, including teachers, knew much of anything about Indian culture or Indian history, and no one even knew there was anything much to know. As the school superintendent my father's dream was to save the brightest Indian students from reservation life, to inspire them to escape off to college, but those he had hopes for either never quite left or quickly returned.

Perhaps many of the Indian people in Frazer still maintained their tribal culture. We didn't know what they knew, and never thought to wonder. It was the Cold War fifties and no one talked about Native American cultural heritage or the sacred hoop of life.

Once I did play Cowboys and Indians with Aaron, an Indian kid who was the largest boy in the sixth grade and tough on the basketball court. He and his father played guitar to-

gether and sang "You Are My Sunshine" in the local talent
show, but they didn't place, which made some of the Indian
people angry enough to boo. I'd just unexpectedly won third
place for a trumpet solo, and suddenly felt strange. Most Indians didn't participate in such white-dominated events. But
Aaron and his Dad got up and played. And they were pretty
good, which is probably the highest compliment that could
be paid to anyone in our small-town competition.

Once when Aaron and I rode our bikes back from school
I somehow ended up crossing with him into Indian territory to his home. We parked the bikes and started toward
his house when a loud drunken white man and a bunch of
Indian men and women burst out of the cabin next door.
The white man began urinating in the dusty street. A small
crowd gathered, kids and neighbors, watching silently. The
group from the cabin laughed and carried on, chugging at
their cans of beer before they all reeled back inside.

We played Cowboys and Indians in the concrete foundations of what used to be a house, and at first that was disconcerting, too. I always chose to be an Indian but Aaron
insisted that he was the Indian, and through some dim sense
of protocol I deferred. Even stuck with the less romantic role
of cowboy, in the familiar ritual I was soon oblivious to everything else. We careened among concrete barricades, shot
guns and arrows, ambushed, war-whooped, and died with
thrashing of limbs and anguished final breaths. When the sun
went down we went home to supper, back to our separate
worlds where cowboys and Indians no longer mingled.

The boy in my class I had most in common with was Snake,
a quiet Indian kid with glasses who liked to read. We talked
about books and were just starting to be friends when he
was killed. He lived with his grandparents who were hard

of hearing, and they pulled out in front of a train at the intersection downtown. The news circulated in hushed tones among the kids that Snake had been decapitated. I never knew why he was named Snake, but I missed him.

The only major racial incident that I was aware of was caused by a strange outsider, an elderly ex-minister from somewhere in the Bible Belt whom Dad hired out of desperation. (A challenging part of a superintendent's job in small-town Montana consisted of finding enough live bodies to man the posts in the local schools.) Mr. Knock quickly became "Knob" to us kids, because—if I can accurately explain our logic—you knocked on a door and his head was as bald as a doorknob, with the exception of a few stray hairs on top that he fussed with endlessly.

Knob had a peculiar, ingratiating manner. Mom described encountering him in Glasgow while my brother and I were ransacking the county library. He saw her through the plate glass window of a department store and began bowing to her, backing down the street, bumping into people, until he disappeared from her view. He taught music and ingeniously combined my trumpet lessons with my brother's drum lessons. Both beginners in the fifth and sixth grades, we played together while he conducted. Blat, blat—bang, bang. He exuded a dervish enthusiasm that energized our duets.

Unfortunately Knob was genuinely crazy, sufficiently unbalanced to create enough racial tension to disturb our comfortable equilibrium. Dad and Mr. Cross, the coach, met in the evenings that week for animated discussions while I huddled in front of the heater in the living room pretending to read, savoring their words as unobtrusively as possible. Some Indian students had finally come to Dad's office to complain. Knob called them "black bastards" in class.

When Dad called him in Knob explained that he called Indian students black bastards because that's exactly what they were. Dad fired him. He lived in the local dormitory, which housed Indian students from outlying areas as well as some of the faculty, including Mr. Cross, who was worried that Knob would set the building on fire, or that the local Indian population would lynch him, or both.

Knob's climactic assault occurred in the school cafeteria, which already seemed to me an impressive dramatic arena. There I first grudgingly recognized eighth grader Bill Waters as an authentic disreputable hero. He was from a tough, white, motherless clan, including his father and older brother along with their Mexican hands. They all cleared heavy brushland down on the Missouri river, and Waters's heroic identity was first suggested to me when he limped in school because of an ax wound.

A favorite game among the boys consisted of loosening the caps of the massive salt and pepper shakers, so that they would come off and ruin the victim's lunch, and Waters had been the victim. His macaroni and cheese was covered an inch thick with pepper. He removed the pepper shaker lid from his plate, never pausing in conversation, never acknowledging what had happened, and proceeded to eat his lunch. We snickerers at the far end of the table quieted down and watched, impressed.

Later Waters stole my first novel—written in pencil when the sixth-grade teacher wasn't looking—about trouble brewing at Mickey Mouse's ranch, with Black Bart rustling somewhere in the background. I didn't think anyone knew about my rapidly proliferating Western romance inspired by comics with book-length stories. But he'd observed me writing in my Indian Head tablet when the teacher wasn't looking and swiped it from my desk. At recess he began reading it to a howling crowd on the playground, while I chased after him in the snow trying to get it back, my broken glasses sliding off my face. Such was the fate of sensitive artists in our rough reservation town.

But the cafeteria's most dramatic confrontation occurred when Knob smashed his lunch tray, loaded with hot potatoes and gravy, over Sam Skinner's head. This was especially shocking because Sam was such an unusually mature and dignified kid, the best basketball player on the junior high school basketball team, who had already established a reputation within the Indian community as a gifted fancy dancer.

The other students didn't know that Mr. Knob had been fired. When Sam sat down next to him his tray slipped, and a bit of gravy slopped on Knob's sleeve. The lunchroom chaos came to a halt as Knob slowly rose, his bald head turning purple with rage. The hot potatoes and gravy exploded over Sam's head into the hair of the plump eighth-grade girl facing me. She couldn't see what was happening but was frozen in the ominous hush, creating a curiously vivid tableau in my memory—the girl's eyes popping out, gravy running down Sam's face, Knob trembling and livid, the lunchroom stilled, like a stop-frame of a movie.

Mr. Cross followed Knob into the bathroom, where blood splattered on the sinks as Knob raved about how the black bastard had made him cut his hand on the broken tray. In the hushed lunchroom we savored our potatoes and gravy and the unexpected drama. That night the county sheriff hauled Knob away before any further violence could erupt. We all settled back into our routines, once again comfortably oblivious to the other world across the street.

Frazer Lake

The lake was stagnant and shallow, a breeding ground for stunted bullheads coated with slime and listless, hog-like carp. My mother never was enthusiastic about the stringers of bullheads I brought home, and she never learned to cook them properly. At least that was my explanation for their odd taste. Bullheads were an unnatural intrusion on her repertoire of fried chicken and roasts and potatoes and gravy. I knew they were excellent fare on the authority of the Miller family, who consumed them in large quantities. But the Millers were a family of recently transplanted Okies who had generations of experience with catfish and southern river fish. They skinned the bullheads and fried them in cornmeal.

To my family, including me, the bullheads tasted strange. Eating them I thought of silt suspended in the warm, placid water of the lake, and they left a lingering taste of mud—food such as the first carnivorous amphibians might have savored, foraging in the ancient, inland sea that once covered the Great Plains. I was always surprised to discover how unappetizing my prize fish turned out to be once they arrived on the dinner table, but I kept bringing them home, emblems of something I cherished but couldn't explain. For me at the age of twelve, poised between childhood and the imminent frenzy of adolescence, Frazer Lake was what the Mississippi was to Huck Finn—the heart of Nature, with all its potent mystery and savage magic.

The walk to Frazer Lake was an adventure in itself, a quest that took me, Phil, and our friends to a timeless center in the wilderness. We began among white frame houses, but a few hundred yards down those gravel streets we entered the Indian section of town, where abandoned cars and dogs proliferated among the asymmetrical angles of log houses. We waved to Indian friends from school as we passed, until the houses thinned out and we trudged through mud holes formed by artesian springs, the invigorating medicinal smell of the water and the fervent whir of grasshoppers heavy in the heat of the day.

After the walk out the beach was an oasis from the road and the summer sun. There we cast our lines loaded with heavy sinkers and bait and sought shade from the dreamy heat as we waited for a bite. What the fish lacked in style they partially made up for in quantity. We arrived home late in the evening, our stringers lined with the spiny, bearded faces of bullheads that still gulped for air in their stolid, primeval determination to survive.

Though I prized the ungainly bullheads, I found the lake's carp population sinister and revolting. On hot afternoons they rose in schools to wallow at the surface. I was ferocious as I waded out to hunt them. Holding my stick above my head, I cautiously approached the dark snouts roiling there in front of me, watching them disappear with uncharacteristic quickness as I brought the stick down with a furious smash, only to hear an empty splat on the warm, silty water.

Once I actually killed one. It thrashed wildly into the air as the stick thunked into it. I clamped down on the floundering, stunned body, then left it to rot there on the beach like the other discarded carp, the snout still writhing as I walked away, feeling savagely victorious but disgusted with the carp, my surroundings, myself. I threw the stick into the marsh. The carp gaped there in the sun. The lake simmered, bubbling slowly as schools of carp continued to gurgle in the afternoon heat.

Now I know it was not a beautiful lake. No tourists stopped there on the way to the trout streams and mountain vistas of the Rockies to the west. The few sandy beaches of Frazer Lake were littered with broken bottles, old worm cans, and rotting carp. Much of the shore was mud that oozed and slurped at your ankles, with an odor of decay. The one unassailable virtue of Frazer Lake was that it was there. It was smelly, unlovely, and its fish were not glamorous. But it had trees, a place to swim, and a beach to daydream on.

In the plains of northeastern Montana such things are luxuries in any form. Any large body of water is a blessing and a mystery, a tropical outpost in that boundless empire of granite rock and sage, stormy skies and wind. To the small reservation town it bordered, the lake seemed as unalterable and reassuring as a womb—an ancient murk of ooze and slime that might have given birth to the first groping motions of life, where time was suspended, like silt in water, while my childhood ended.

Cruising Main

The north side of Froid's Main Street belongs to the kids. Their territory is two blocks of sidewalk stretching from the D&D "Dog Den" Café to the Lutheran church across the street from the old movie theater (open only on summer weekends).

The adults have the south side of Main Street. The two bars are there and parents traffic all night between them, until the late hours come and the last parties form up and pile into cars. Driving a little recklessly now, they cruise thirty-five miles north to Plentywood for steaks and dancing at the Blue Moon Inn. They drift boozily back to high school days on the way. Bottles of beer are tilted up, drained, flung out the window with a nostalgic, familiar flourish. Old stories come to life again, shouted out between front seat and back above the drone of the engine.

We are the high school kids, who've graduated from the Dog Den to cars. We occupy the two blocks of Main Street, one of asphalt, one still gravel. Our cars move in a slow, dreamlike procession, honking acknowledgement each time they meet in the endless ellipse from curb to curb while we inside hold our beer cans and cigarettes below the level of the windows, raising them only at the corner of the curb where we can't quite be seen.

Since it's early we still care that we're on display, still play it cool to our audience of parents and younger kids. We wait for the delirious camaraderie that comes when our cars gather east of town at Herminson's old granaries.

Now, cruising Main, just beginning to feel the mellow glow of the beer, we're still a little careful and grim, still shaking off our Saturday night starched awkwardness. We're still adjusting to the fact that we are the ones inside the cars at last, flipping beer cans like the seniors we remember when we were those gangly thirteen-year-olds on the church steps, when we, too, watched our futures cruise by in the arrogant arc of lobbed beer cans, the fierce spin-out of '57 Chevies at the curb, and dreamed again the short-lived glamour of those gravel streets.

Boom and Bust

"Son, I'm going to have to ask you to put out the cigar."

Every face in the Greyhound bus turned back to look at me, sitting precisely in the center of the back row of seats, exhaling smoke for the first time. Thank God he stopped me after the second puff, or I'd have gotten sick. Some of the faces looked amused, others exasperated and astounded. I'm not sure why I thought that no one would notice a twelve-year-old boy lighting up a cigar in the back of a bus, and I hadn't anticipated how the odor of the cheroot would turn the heads and wrinkle the noses of everyone near me. I quickly stubbed out the cigar in the nearest ashtray and put it in my pocket.

The cigar was an experiment, I suppose, to test the limits of my sudden freedom and prosperity. I was more than a bit scared, but mainly I was giddy at the prospect of traveling alone for the first time, with money in my billfold and no adults along to supervise me. Uncle Phil and Aunt Roma had put me on the bus in Rupert, Idaho, and I was due to arrive in my new home of Froid thirty-six hours later, after riding nearly a thousand miles across southern Idaho, up western Montana, and east across the Hi-Line to the far corner of the state. We'd made our first rest stop in Pocatello and for some reason I'd decided that this would be a good time to try smoking a cigar, so I bought a bottle of pop, a paperback science fiction novel off the bookrack, and the exotic looking wine-soaked crook cheroot, before piling back on the bus.

By the time we arrived in Great Falls the next morning I felt like an experienced traveler. I'd ordered a cheeseburger and fries for dinner the night before, slept off and on while trying to find a comfortable position in the bus seat during the long night, and had just finished my sausage and eggs breakfast at the hotel restaurant where our bus had let us out. Ordering and paying for my own meals at restaurants had left me feeling newly mature and confident, as memories of faces glaring at me through cigar smoke faded. I asked the waitress for a refill of my coffee cup, looking forward to curling up in the hotel lobby to read my science fiction novel during the six-hour layover, waiting for the next bus heading north.

"Is David Mogen here?" the bus driver called out. I swiveled on the café stool and waved, and he walked over to me. "They need to talk to you at the Greyhound bus desk. There's a problem with your connection."

"How old are you?" the bus manager asked, seeming surprised to discover that I was a kid.

"Twelve." I hated the fact that I apparently looked young for my age.

"I'm sorry. This never should have happened," he explained. "They sold you a ticket to take you from Havre to Culbertson, and we just discontinued our service on that route yesterday. We'll refund your money for the ticket, of course, but you'll have to arrange some other way to get there."

Suddenly I felt like a scared kid hundreds of miles from home. Even though Aunt Roma and Uncle Phil had come to seem like my second set of parents, sometimes it had seemed strange to work so far from home all summer, and the home

I was traveling to now wasn't even the one I'd left. I suddenly felt stranded with a dwindling supply of travel money in a big city.

"What should I do?" I asked.

"Well, we can try to get you a seat on a train, but you might have to spend a night or two in Havre. Do you have someone you can call?"

"My family is in Froid, up by Plentywood. They were going to pick me up in Culbertson."

"You'd better call them." He looked embarrassed and concerned. "You can use the pay phone in the corner."

When the operator got through I carefully deposited change after I heard Mom answer. "Mom, I'm here in Great Falls but they say they can't take me any farther than Havre."

"Well, I never heard of anything so ridiculous," she spluttered, after I explained what had happened. "After they sold you the ticket and you're still hundreds of miles from home, now they tell us? Harold, it's David. You'd better talk to him."

Dad sounded almost amused by the absurdity of the situation, as I explained that I wouldn't get to Havre until that evening and didn't know whether to try to get a train ticket.

"Well, maybe I can get there in time to meet you. Don't worry, I'll pick you up at the bus station."

And shortly after I arrived he was there, after driving west all afternoon along the Hi-Line. He bought us supper and listened as I filled him in on my recent adventures, except for the incident with the cheroot. I told him the story of my summer. I was tan and strong from striding along ditch banks with a shovel, working in water and mud, and from long days walking up and down rows of potatoes and sugar beets with a hoe, chopping weeds.

"*Mas agua*," José would say, straightening up to lean on his hoe and reach for his canteen, surveying the broad green rows of potatoes.

"*Mas agua*," I would agree, chugging at my canteen. More water. I had learned four words of Spanish while working with him, and they were all functional.

"*Mucho yedova*," I would proclaim, after assessing our progress. Many weeds. Mostly pigweed, carpeting the soil beneath the potatoes, weeds whose tangled roots were easy to miss when you were trying to move fast. My back was almost black from working shirtless, crouched over the hoe while walking up and down the long rows in the summer sun.

"*Mucho yedova*," José would agree as he recapped his canteen. He was the father of a Mexican migrant family that returned every summer to work in the fields, and he worked at such a firm and steady pace that I had to push myself hard to keep up. I'd coach him in English sometimes during our lunch break, and though we didn't speak much of the same language, I'd come to feel comfortable with him. He worked hard without unnecessary strain, and moved with a quiet dignity I admired.

I'd made a sport of trying to match his dexterity at slashing weeds on either side while maintaining a consistent stride. Olympic Hoeing, I thought, imagining José and I coming down the last row ahead of a Soviet team, while trumpets blared and the crowd roared. "The U.S. has won Gold at last," the announcer proclaimed on the radio broadcast, conveniently ignoring the fact that José was actually Mexican.

Such fantasies were consistent with my strategy for surviving the summer in style. I'd grown up hearing Dad's stories about ferocious work during the Depression for small pay or even just room and board, and as I began working at my first real job I realized that I wanted a reputation not just as a good worker but as a great worker. My summer of heroically busting my butt paid off when I heard Uncle Phil describe me to Dad on the phone as "the hardest working kid I've ever seen." I was proud of the compliment but dimly realized, as I returned to the fields the next day, that I was now saddled with expectations I'd now have to live up to and might someday regret.

But on this night at least I knew Dad was proud of me as I rambled on, demonstrating my firsthand knowledge of irrigated farming while finishing my chicken-fried steak. He shook out some tobacco from his bag of Bull Durham, rolled a cigarette, then reached into his sport coat pocket and pulled out what appeared to be a small black cylinder.

"What's that?" I asked. To save money he'd given up Camels for his old Bull Durham years ago, back in Whitewater, and I'd always admired his cigarette-rolling technique. He'd once shown Phil and me how to roll them one-handed, like you would while holding reins and sheltering against the wind on horseback, and we were impressed.

"It's a cigarette holder." He inserted the cigarette in the end and lit up, blowing the smoke out in a circle that drifted in front of us. "This way I can get filters without paying for those fancy new brands." He opened it up to show me how you could insert a new filter when the old one got dirty. Except for some old-timers it was rare to see anyone smoking Bull Durham cigarettes anymore, and Dad was the only one I've ever seen who smoked them in a cigarette holder. He enjoyed telling the story about the surprised reactions of other school administrators at an NEA convention in Atlantic City when they observed him rolling his own cigarettes.

It was dark when we got in the car, and I was suddenly comfortable and reassured as I slid into the familiar seat with Dad at the wheel. He woke me as the first light of dawn began to break in the east.

"We're almost to Culbertson," he said. "Then it's just fifteen miles north to Froid. I thought you might want to see the town that's our big rival."

"So Culbertson and Froid are rivals?" I was suddenly alert.

"That's all you hear about there. How we have to beat Culbertson this year in basketball."

Between working all summer in Idaho and the excitement of my trip, I really hadn't focused much on the fact that I would soon be arriving in another new home. Frazer was in the same Class C conference as Froid and Culbertson, so for the past three years I'd come to know them from watching their visiting basketball teams, which usually battled for the conference championship.

"Population 432" declared the sign next to the road leading into Froid. More than twice the size of Frazer, and more than five times the population of Whitewater. And of course the actual community included all the farming families within a fifteen-mile radius. I was just entering the eighth grade, suddenly bracing myself once more for the testing that goes with being the oldest kid of the new school superintendent.

When we arrived Mom got everyone up and was already cooking bacon and eggs and fried potatoes as I hugged my younger brothers and sisters, then let them eagerly escort me upstairs to show me the room that I would share with Phil in the back end of one of the newly constructed attic bedrooms. It was a small home for a family of eight, with only one bathroom, but there was an ice rink behind the house, and we were just a block from the school and the playground.

"Maybe you should go get a haircut from that barber downtown," Mom said a few days later, handing me a five-dollar bill. I was amazed. Until then Dad had always cut our hair. He wasn't a stylist, but he prided himself on precision. "How long do you want it?" he would ask, and once you specified a length he'd try to get every hair on your head to meet the standard. Mom must have decided it was worth an investment to get me started right in a new school.

I strolled the three blocks to downtown, enjoying the breeze and the shade from the big trees in late August. After working all summer I realized how much I'd loved the summers of my childhood, the three months of pure freedom, when I could play basketball with Phil and whoever else was around at the school playground, or walk out to the lake to fish, or read all day if I felt like it. (Once in Frazer I calculated that I had read six books that day since early morning, as I finally turned off the light at midnight.) It was nice to relax a bit during this last lull before school started, finding my way around in my new hometown.

Mom looked me over as I walked back into the kitchen and handed her the two dollars I'd received in change. "Well, it looks good. Nancy Miller told me he does a good job."

She was lifting hot chocolate chip cookies with a spatula from a baking pan to a plate. I eagerly got a glass of milk and sat down at the table to sample them. Dad and the other kids were gone, so it was a rare interlude, speaking to her without distraction from the usual family chaos.

"I got a shave too," I announced, savoring the gooey warmth of my first bite.

"A shave?" She paused, spatula in hand.

"Well, yeah." I laughed a bit nervously. She was looking at me contemplatively, as though seeing me for the first time. "I noticed I had a little bit of hair above my lip, so I thought since I was at a barbershop I might as well get it shaved off too. It was weird though. He sharpened this big razor on a leather strap and smeared me with hot lather he made up in a cup. I didn't dare move."

She put the spatula down slowly. "Was anyone else there?"

"Some high school kid. He was reading magazines. I guess he was next. Don Dubner, I think his name was. The barber introduced us."

She seemed to be contemplating something other than my freshly cut hair and shaved upper lip, which suddenly seemed sensitive and exposed.

"That Dubner boy will tell everyone in town," she said, as much to herself as to me. She put a fresh cookie on my plate, poured herself another cup of coffee, lit a cigarette, and exhaled the smoke with a soft sigh, as she gazed out the kitchen window.

"Well, you might hear about this next week in school," she finally observed. "Just be prepared."

Something about the way she said it brought back bits of memory in a new way. The appraising glint in the barber's eyes as I showed him the first signs of fuzz above my upper lip. A kind of shudder in Don Dubner's spine as he lifted the magazine he was reading up in front of his face. Well, this is the country where Mom grew up, I realized. She seemed tuned in somehow, an oracle delivering a riddle I'd have to figure out myself.

I'd forgotten all about the haircut and shave by the time school began. Froid seemed fast-paced and wild compared to the other towns we'd lived in, partly because it was bigger and more prosperous, and partly because in entering the eighth grade I was experiencing the first convulsions of adolescence while trying to figure out how to fit in to another new town.

I was strolling over to the school playground when a girl called out to me from the doorway of Mr. Randall's house. He was the high school science teacher who had come by our home to visit a few days earlier.

"Hey," she said, stepping out from behind the screen door. "Are you the new superintendent's boy?"

"Yeah, my name's David," I stammered as I walked over to shake her hand. "David Mogen."

"I'm Paula," she said, as another girl stepped through the door to join us. "And this is Janette." Paula was a brunette with a pony tail, and Janette was a bouncy blonde. They were both cute.

"Hi," said Janette as we shook hands. "What grade are you in?"

"Eighth. What about you?"

"We're both in your class," proclaimed Paula. "Come on in. We're babysitting for Mr. and Mrs. Randall. You can have some of my Coke." I followed them through the door, saying hello to the two-year-old. The baby was asleep in the crib. They filled me in about the town and our class until the

Randalls came home and paid them. After we all said good-bye the girls and I stepped outside and chatted a bit more before I turned to continue my walk.

"Hey, I'll see you in school. Thanks for the Coke."

"Where are you going?" asked Paula.

"Oh, just to the playground to see if anything's happening. Maybe downtown if no one's there."

"We're coming with you," announced Janette.

"Oh that's all right. I'll see you later." I felt like I was suddenly involved in a game where I didn't know the rules. "See you."

I turned and trotted away, but when I looked back I discovered that they were trotting along behind me. I picked up my pace and headed down the street, feeling foolish and a bit panicky. They stayed right with me. I ran fast to the last block on the west end of town and to my amazement they were still right behind me, Paula's pony tail flying straight out behind her.

"Damn, these girls can run," I thought, as I kicked into high gear, heading towards the stockyards west of town. I was small for my age but wiry and quick, and one thing I could do was run when I got into open space. I broke into a full sprint, did a dodge and weave through the stockyard, imagining I was breaking free on a kickoff return, and angled over towards the big granaries by the railroad track. When I finally slowed down to look back I saw that they had stopped by the stockyard and seemed to be giggling.

I dodged back into an alley and came out on Main Street by the Annex Bar, then trudged slowly up the three blocks to home, trying to figure out why they'd started chasing me and why I ran. I never did figure it out.

School was fun, actually. My seventh-and-eighth-grade class was bigger than any I'd been in, and there was a lot of energy in the school. Phil and I were used to being the class "brains"—except in art, at which we were both hopeless—but to my relief I'd discovered that here we shared the role with other kids. Since Dad's office was right by the door entering the school, it seemed a bit like home, and I was getting along with everyone so far.

Three other eighth-grade boys and I were standing by the gym door after lunch, joking around, while some of the high school boys came up the stairs. They stopped and looked us over.

"A pretty clean-shaven crew, wouldn't you say?" observed Pete Randolph. I knew their names and reputations as athletes by now.

"Yeah, this Mogen kid sure doesn't have any whiskers. He looks like he gets shaved professionally," said Ron Lamarre, reaching out to stroke my lip.

His older brother Bob wasn't much of a talker, but I could tell he was the leader. He was one of those kids who looked like a grown man as a senior. Even though he was less than six feet tall he played center on the basketball team because he had a broad, muscular body that could move people around inside and he had a sure instinct about when to shoot or pass from the post. He glared down at me.

"So I hear you go to the barber to get shaved."

Somewhere in the back of my mind I had heeded Mom's warning and tried to prepare, but I hadn't come up with any strategy that made sense except to take my medicine and try not to make things worse.

"Well, I did once."

He grabbed my right forearm with his meat-grinder hands and slowly began to twist, scowling. "Keep those whiskers off. We don't want you young punks to make the school look bad." They hovered over me as I stared straight ahead, ignoring the pain. Bob Lamarre snarled as he dropped my arm before they sauntered down the hall, breaking up in laughter.

"Geez, did you really ask the barber for a shave?" asked Steve, who was becoming my best friend. He and Arnie and Vic were chuckling nervously now, too. I shrugged hopelessly. Obviously everyone knew the story, and there wasn't anything I could say that wouldn't just make it sound more ridiculous.

After a few months the shaving story grew old and the teasing tapered off. Dad seemed to be popular, even though he and the new coach began enforcing training rules and suspended a football player for smoking, in a program where kids had previously smoked inside the locker room. But things settled down and most people seemed to welcome the change. Mr. Randall and some of the other new teachers Dad had hired were enthusiastic and smart. Phil and Doris and I were all in the school band, which included anyone from the fifth grade up who was willing and able to take up an instrument, so our day started at band practice before classes. Our home was filled with the sounds of band instruments as well as of the used piano Mom had invested in.

By my sophomore year Phil and I had started to prove ourselves in the arena that mattered most to the community— sports. We quickly became "the Mogen boys" to the coaches and town, lumped together for praise or blame, and mostly that had worked out pretty well.

I was backup quarterback, handing off to Phil at halfback, and I was discovering that backup quarterback in eight-man football at a small school is a demanding position. The first team consisted of physically mature juniors and seniors, tough farm kids who outweighed my young offensive line on the second team by about forty pounds to a man. I was 135 pounds wringing wet, and I'd come to see my job as trying to get a play under way before getting mauled.

"Hut one, hut two, hut three," I'd bark, and then I'd try to hang onto the ball as my line collapsed and I was swarmed under. My right guard, Puggy, still had baby fat and was so awkward he could barely get down into stance. I'd hear him yelping at the bottom of the pile as the defensive linemen gleefully pinched his soft flesh. I gutted it out as best I could, triumphant when I could just get the ball out of my hands so somebody else would get tackled.

But basketball was the one universal religion in that country, back before televised college and pro games competed for attention with the hometown teams. In the home game against Culbertson that year Phil really established us as a part of the community. Several of our starters had fouled out, and with five minutes to go the coach told him to check in. We were down by six, and the gym was so packed that latecomers craned through the door above the stairs trying to see. The crowd stood and screamed throughout the second half, as Culbertson slowly pulled out ahead. Phil was just a freshman and didn't have any offense, but in practice he'd already established himself as a quick, fierce defender, so the coach put him in for the first time under pressure in the biggest game of the year. He stole the ball twice down the stretch, and we won the game at the buzzer.

"We think you and Phil are just great," Mrs. Miller exclaimed to me outside the grocery later that week. Happy to bask in my brother's glory, I realized that our time had come, the time that boys in small towns everywhere began dreaming of when they were barely big enough to dribble.

When we lived in Box Elder we kids would listen, enraptured, to the radio broadcasts of the district basketball tournament, while all the adults in town were up in Havre at the games. I'd make up games afterward, racing back and forth shooting a crumpled piece of paper into a wastebasket on the porch while announcing the play-by-play broadcasts of the fantasy Box Elder Bearcubs elementary school team, starring Phil and me, as it ascended to national and international prominence, finally beating a Soviet team to win the world championship.

Now it was starting. In the next few years we'd finally enter the theater that kids in small towns dreamed about during their long years playing sports until dark at the school playground, the years that parents in the community remembered from their own glory days back in high school.

During my junior year we actually beat Culbertson in football, an event that could not compare to the importance of a win in basketball, which could shape the town's perception of whether it was a good or bad year, but seemed monumental in its own way because it was so unprecedented. Though Froid was always strong in basketball, for some reason we had never been any good in football. But that year we had a large athletic senior class, and some of us younger players had matured. Even Puggy had slimmed down and muscled up.

I was starting at quarterback and defensive back by now, and Phil played halfback and middle linebacker. We both returned punts and kickoffs and played coverage on defense on special teams. If you were a starter you never came off the field unless you were injured or too cramped-up to stand, so everyone on the field from both teams was exhausted from playing all afternoon in the broiling early fall sun. We were actually trying to hold a lead at the end of the game, having driven the length of the field for a go-ahead touchdown to open the fourth quarter.

They were running a final play from the three-yard line, trying to score the winning touchdown, as the clock ran out. One of their star twin running backs broke to the outside as all the blockers entangled inside, so I was the only tackler left between him and the goal. This was one of those moments I'd fantasized about as a kid, but when it came I was so tired I could barely move or think. He tried to make a stutter step, which would have worked because I had no energy to make an adjustment, but I could see from his pale, drawn face that he didn't have the energy to complete the move, and we collapsed into each other at the two-yard line as the whistle blew to end the game. The Froid crowd standing along the sidelines applauded, delirious with surprise, as we shook hands with the Culbertson team and straggled to the school bus to head back home.

"Goddamn it, we finally beat Culberston," yelled Mike Ritter, our star senior halfback, as we staggered into the bus and began stripping off tape and sweat-soaked jerseys. The coaches giddily walked up and down the aisle slapping us on the back, recounting key plays.

The stories had begun. No one thought we'd ever really beat Culbertson in football, but now it had happened. We'd done it. It wasn't winning the district basketball championship with a radio broadcast immortalizing every move to the known world, but it was definitely a moment of glory to live up to some of my childhood dreams.

After we returned to Froid and showered a bunch of us piled into the family station wagon and headed south to Culbertson to celebrate. It was Saturday night and the town was buzzing after the game. Everyone knew Dad's Chevy station wagon, and we'd stop and yell stories back and forth to other cars filled with Froid kids celebrating in enemy territory, while carloads of kids from Culbertson honked their horns and waved their arms out the window, flipping us off in rage. Life was perfect. We were exhausted warriors with stories to share, and everyone wanted to hear them.

Mike Ritter hollered out the window to some older guys I didn't really know, and then turned from the window to ask, "Hey, do you all want to go to the fish camp? They want us to come down to the river and celebrate."

The fish camp. I'd heard of it, but never imagined I'd see it. Somewhere down by the Missouri River, tended by some old-timers who kept fresh fish in supply and cooked them up for men who arrived with cases of beer to play poker and eat fried catfish and ling with hash browns. We followed them down the dirt roads to the river, shouting out our victory stories as we bounced over the rough road. When we got there the older guys carried in the cases of beer and stacked them on the table. One of them pulled out a bottle of blackberry brandy and placed it on top of the beer.

"I'll bet none of you can drink this without taking it down from your lips," he proclaimed.

I picked up the bottle, twisted off the lid, and began to glug it down. Everyone watched, transfixed. I'd never drunk much alcohol, except for an occasional swallow of beer or sip of whiskey shared by adults at dinner parties, and based on my limited experience with hard liquor I expected the brandy to be undrinkable after the first swallow or two. I was surprised to discover that it actually chugged down easily, like heavy fruit juice that created a pleasant burn in my stomach.

I swigged until there were only a few swallows left, then gasped for air as I slammed the bottle down. I felt ecstatically invigorated for a few minutes, then shaky and queasy. No one seemed to know what to say, except to point out that since the bottle wasn't empty I really hadn't won the dare. About ten minutes later I stepped outside and started vomiting.

I don't remember much about the meal and cards, and when we headed back home Phil drove, while I huddled in the far corner of the back seat, semi-delirious and smelling of blackberry vomit. Our head coach, backed by Dad, had made it clear over the past few years that the newly enforced training rules required observing training hours as well as giving up drinking and smoking. In celebration of our victory the coaches had extended the Saturday night hours from midnight to one, so when we left before midnight we had plenty of time to get home before the deadline. I might even have been able to stumble up the stairs without our parents noticing, if they were asleep.

Except for the train.

Out in the middle of nowhere in the middle of the night, blocking the dirt-road entrance to the camp, was a train. There was no way around it, no way to know why it was stopped there or when it would move. We sat there in Dad's station wagon until nearly three in the morning, when it slowly began to pull away. The streets were empty when we arrived in Froid, but as we approached the main intersection a familiar figure shuffled out from under the streetlight to block our path.

"Shit, it's Henry," breathed Mike Ritter. "Let us out of here."

Phil pulled over so that he and the others could slide out the doors and run, then drove down the street, stopped, and rolled down his window.

Henry the Cop loomed outside talking to Phil, while I slumped miserably in the back seat hoping he wouldn't speak to me.

"Your Dad called the Highway Patrol a couple of hours ago to put out a search for you. He was sure you wouldn't have broken training rules, so he figured something must have happened."

"Oh, geez, he would think that," said Phil. "We went to the fish camp down by the river and couldn't get out because a train sat there all night blocking the tracks." We could both hear how absurd the story sounded, and even in my diminished state of mind I shuddered to imagine telling it to Dad.

"Uh huh," said Henry. "Well, you'd better get on home. I imagine your dad's still up waiting for news."

He was. He stood in front of the heat vent rubbing his hands with a look of exasperated disbelief while Phil haltingly explained about the train. I tried to remain inconspicuous in the background.

"What's the matter with you?" Dad asked, focusing on me for the first time. He stepped toward me and stopped. "You're drunk."

I couldn't think of anything to say. I could barely stand, and he obviously could smell as well as see my condition.

He turned back to stand in front of the heat vent, looking us over thoughtfully. "Well, you're both off the team."
There was nothing further to discuss. I'm not sure Dad ever
believed our story about the train, to his dying day.

Dad and the coaches assembled the team on Monday to
explain to them why Phil and I had been dismissed. Since
we were no longer team members we weren't allowed at the
meeting, and only heard about it through our friends.

"We told them you guys weren't any worse than some of
the rest of us," Mike Ritter recounted. "That you just got
caught because you were his sons. He said that if any of the
rest of us broke the rules we should be suspended too."

We watched the television news from Williston, the one
station that served the entire northeast corner of Montana as
well as the northwest corner of North Dakota. "The football
coach and superintendent in Froid have cancelled the Class
C championship game with Savage," he announced. "They
suspended two starters in the backfield for breaking training rules, and felt that under the circumstances they can't
compete effectively."

We'd lost a couple of other players to injury, and Savage had
already beaten us badly during the regular season when we
were at full strength, so our coach had decided to just throw
in the towel. Savage had a kid named Jack Heller, who in
our small-town eight-man football league was like Superman
playing in his cape. He was over six feet tall, weighed 225
pounds of solid muscle, and was the fastest, strongest player
anyone could remember. At the district track tournament
he scored over fifty points by himself, twice as many as the
second-place team, winning all the sprints and strength events
he could fit into his schedule. He was actually recruited by

some major colleges, including Notre Dame, but had no interest in doing anything after high school except working on the family farm and partying.

In my most vivid memory of Heller we were trying to stop a final drive before the half, and I had resolved that if he came my way I'd hit him with every ounce of strength at my command to make certain he didn't score. I decided it would be a test of my theory that a person could do pretty much anything through complete concentration of mind and will. I met him with a picture-perfect tackle at the knees at the three-yard line and I'm not certain he even knew I was there. Splat! I was laid out prostrate on the ground, feeling like a flattened cartoon character, as he sprinted through me into the end zone.

The announcer launched into a short speech after delivering the rest of the sports news, commending the coaches and administration in Froid for placing ethics above winning. Everyone in the area knew that the suspended players were the superintendent's sons.

I felt that I'd never be able to forgive myself for the wounded look in Dad's eyes that night, but as time passed and I entered my senior year I realized that the community, even Dad himself, had accepted and forgiven us. In fact I wondered if we weren't even more accepted, as though we had endured some secret rite of passage that granted us officially unacknowledged stature. It was only a football championship after all, not a basketball game against a rival. And drinking too much was something people understood.

In a state that seemed to cherish a reputation for hard drinking, the northeastern Hi-Line more than held its own.

I heard reference several times to an article in *Life* magazine back in the 1950s that had cited our region as consuming the most beer per capita of any in the country. On a national scale that seemed to count as our fifteen minutes of fame, and I sometimes wondered if we all participated in an unacknowledged competition to preserve our standing.

Phil and I never broke training rules again, but when the sports seasons ended we eagerly joined in the ongoing scramble among high school kids in the area to talk older friends and acquaintances into serving as bootleggers. We trailed them to bars up and down the line from Culbertson to Plentywood, negotiating to buy cases of beer and anything else containing alcohol that we could get our hands on. Beer cans flew out of the car windows at escalating speeds as the parties careened up and down the highways.

Everyone gathered at Herminson's granaries east of town to swap stories and beer, before blasting back to cruise Main Street. By evening, when the reception improved, our cars throbbed with the latest hit tunes crooning in from KOMA in Oklahoma City. Elvis, Little Richard, Jerry Lee Lewis, tragic teen-romance ballads like "Teen Angel" and "She Was Only Seventeen." Parents partied all night in the bars, we high school kids partied in our cars, and kids too young to drive or ride looked on from the street or the D&D Café while we made the slow circle up and down the three blocks of Main Street. There was lots of vitality in our community, I realized, and on nights and weekends it centered around bars and cars.

"It doesn't sound good," Dad observed a year later. I couldn't respond because the dentist had my mouth pried open as he set my front teeth back in place. We were in Wolf Point, listening to our team lose a Saturday morning elimination game at the divisional tournament, the final game of my high school career.

We'd all had legs of lead that morning, after playing back-to-back evening games on Thursday and Friday, but we were ahead in the second quarter when I wrestled for a rebound with a big forward from Outlook, whose elbow smashed in my front teeth. Dad and the coaches escorted me off the floor, spitting blood into a towel as my tongue probed the teeth sticking straight back into my mouth.

I'd never had a serious injury before, except for a concussion in a football game in Richey, a condition that at that time was called "getting your bell rung" and was not taken seriously. I'd actually finished the game, though I never could quite remember coming back to win in overtime. And now I was suddenly transported from the noisy tournament arena I'd spent my childhood dreaming of getting to, listening above the whine of the dentist's drill to the radio broadcast of my team playing its last game.

Boom and bust. The radio broadcaster chronicled our team's final desperate surge to come from behind. My best friend Steve, as usual, led all scorers. A sophomore kid who would go on to become a star had taken my place and made some big shots down the stretch, but we were down too far by then to come back.

"Well, it's all over," observed Dad, as the announcers began their introduction to the next game. "I thought you guys might get to the state tournament. It's too bad it had to end like this for you." The dentist was applying some kind of moist plaster gunk around my teeth to hold them in place. "But you had a helluva good year."

And it had been a good year, I thought. But it was all over

now. The curtain had just come down on the theater of high
school sports that had dominated our lives for the past few
years, and I wasn't even on stage. It had been a great senior
year, all things considered. We'd had another winning season in football, and Phil had established himself as one of
the most valuable players in the conference now that Heller
and the previous year's senior class were gone. We'd won the
conference championship in basketball and gotten to the divisional tournament in Wolf Point and almost made it to the
state tournament in Billings. But it was all ended now, and
in months to come as I became increasingly preoccupied by
fantasies about moving to Columbia University on Manhattan Island, I also contemplated in a new way this Hi-Line
country I would soon leave behind.

Boom and bust. As I looked back on all the stories I'd grown
up with, I seemed to see a pattern. Bust your butt to make a
dream come true, and then either watch it blow up, or screw
it up yourself.

I had no idea why I suddenly decided to ask for a shave after my first haircut in a barber shop. But I did. I'd never exactly decided to glug down the bottle of blackberry brandy,
as far as I could recall. But I did it. The broken teeth in my
last game weren't my fault, but they seemed part of a fatal-
ity I couldn't fathom, part of a story I seemed to participate
in without exactly choosing it.

Riding the tractor that summer I tried to visualize Columbia and New York City, and I also contemplated my ambivalence toward heroes. They all seemed to have hidden flaws,
and they definitely took their medicine. Even Superman never
got credit, I reflected, because in real life he was just Clark

Kent. And though he always conquered in the end, every victory seemed only to prepare the way for his next defeat.

Closer to home my western heroes all seemed to have a shadow side. You had Gene Autry riding high on Champion, but riding by his side was Gabby Hayes. The homesteader father in *Shane* was a good man, but he never could be a hero like the cowboy gunslinger. And what was the past that haunted Shane, even as he rode off victorious into the sunset? Shane. Shame. They seemed to ride together.

Perhaps we need a superhero called Okay Man, I thought, who jumps into phone booths to strip off his superhero costume and emerges as just a normal guy, not looking for glory or trouble. Everyone could just be okay, without all these boom-and-bust stories. But who would really care to read stories about Okay Man? I was just tired of all the letdowns.

Maybe it's all just about growing up. But even if it is maybe I needed a new kind of hero, I'd think, trying to visualize the "Acropolis of Morningside Heights" described in the Columbia brochures, trying to imagine life in an Ivy League university in the far-away East. Maybe there's some kind of eastern hero who fulfills his dreams without having them go bust or screwing them up. I couldn't think of any, except maybe for a few characters, from some stories I'd read by Henry James, who never seemed content for reasons too subtle for me to make out. A hero in a three-piece brown tweed suit like the one I just bought for college, I thought, as I packed to leave. What would he be like? What would he do? All that came to mind were vague images of prosperous men doing business—lawyers, doctors, maybe professors. But who knew what I would discover?

I was fired up about going to college. During my senior year I'd been reading anthologies of Shakespeare and long

Russian novels just for fun, and I'd assembled a pretty extensive collection of classical music through a record club, which no one knew about except my family and Rob Ray, the band teacher, who would discuss with me what I'd heard and advise me about what to get next. Maybe these things will be important over there, I thought. I can become anything I want. I'm going to a new world, starting over. Maybe I just need new, more substantial dreams. Maybe I'll read all the greatest books ever written, and listen to all the greatest music, and find a new way.

The train was pulling in at the Williston station, and I was saying my last good-byes to the family as it shuddered to a stop. I'd hugged all my younger brothers and sisters, exchanged final slugs in the arm with Phil, and shaken Dad's hand. Mom looked me in the eye after we hugged, and I could see she was holding back tears.

"Write and let us know how you're doing," she said. "Oh, it's so far away. Take care of yourself in that big city."

I found my seat and stored my suitcase, containing my new clothes with the white robe and three-piece tweed suit. I waved to my family from my window as they all waved back while the train slowly gained speed.

The train was moving east across the Great Plains of North Dakota when I remembered that I had a new pipe and tobacco in my pocket that I hadn't tried out yet. After considerable gagging and choking I'd managed to start smoking cigarettes in off-seasons during my last two years, so that I could participate in the rituals of sneaking off to Paul Smevlins's garage at noon to smoke with the other guys, and share the general camaraderie provided by bumming and repaying cigarettes. But I'd recently decided that since I was heading east to college perhaps it was time to try something different, so I'd bought a cheap pipe and some Cherry Blend tobacco, which the drugstore owner assured me was popular and pleasantly aromatic.

I found a relatively secluded seat in the back of a train car. After a few tries with my new cigarette lighter I drew pipe smoke into my lungs for the first time, choking a bit at the strong taste. I settled back in my seat, watching the plains flow by, absorbing the emotions of leaving, and adjusting to the feel of the pipe in my mouth, the sweet heavy aroma of the Cherry Blend.

"Excuse me," said an older college girl sitting up and across the aisle beside her boyfriend, turning to face me as she spoke. Others in the railroad car looked back curiously, hearing the sharp tone in her voice and wrinkling their noses at the spreading aroma of Cherry Blend. "That pipe smoke is really strong. Would you mind putting it out, or going someplace else to smoke it?"

Boom and bust, I thought, as I tamped out the pipe and put it in my pocket, hoping I wasn't blushing with embarrassment. Maybe it will be different when I arrive in New York City. I settled back, resolved to enjoy the journey anyway.

Boom and bust, I reflected dreamily as I gazed out the window while the train blasted east across the plains. Maybe they're my heroes, like it or not. Maybe I'm stuck with them. I pictured Boom, wearing his white hat, astride his white stallion. Strong and resolute, relaxed yet poised, he was prepared for anything. And there trailing behind him, riding a tired old mule, was his companion Bust, wearing his moth-eaten old dark hat and shabby clothes. He looked sick and hung over and his face was bruised, the face of a man who had lost his summer's wages playing poker while drunk, then got the worst of a barroom brawl.

How did these two end up together? I wondered. Maybe they were brothers, or bound together through some story from the past. I sensed that the cocky slant of Boom's hat might set him up for trouble down the road. Maybe he was thinking too much about how and when he could celebrate his good fortune. Bust looked grim but determined, like someone who had learned a lesson and was intent on remembering it. Maybe they sometimes switched roles after their visits to town, I speculated, when Boom gets busted and Bust wins big and reclaims his horse and hat.

The sun was setting on the Great Plains and the clouds spread across the big sky glowed with rosy light. I'm coming to the end of the West, I realized. When we hit the eastern border of North Dakota I'll be farther east then I've ever been, and it will all be behind me. When the sun comes up tomorrow I'll be approaching Chicago, and the East Coast won't be far ahead.

In my mind's eye I saw them riding off into the distance, their figures fading into the dying light. One of them was hunched sideways in his saddle in the wind, rolling and lighting a cigarette with one hand. Let them ride, I thought, just let them ride, reaching into the pocket of my sports coat to feel the heft of my new pipe. Things change. Tomorrow the sun will rise on a new world, and I'll have left Boom and Bust far behind, riding forever in their endless prairie.

I figured I'd meet them again sometime, probably when I least expected it. But for now the train hurtled away from the fading light as I finally drifted off to sleep, trying to imagine the new Acropolis gleaming on the heights above a teeming city.

Closing the Circle

Iniskim

After my father died in June of 1998 I just drifted. Through all the stress and anguish something beautiful had happened that I couldn't fathom. Some story had been completed with my father's death, but I couldn't make out where it began or what it meant or whether it was really finished. I seemed to be pursuing a quest that I didn't understand, musing about his life and my life and the family history in Montana and the way things converged in those last months in Billings while he was dying.

When he was diagnosed as terminal the previous fall the doctors had given him six to twelve months, and he died nine months later. Since we had cared for him the entire time at my brother's home it had been exhausting for everyone in the family and I was worn out. But there was something else going on, something that I could feel but not explain. I returned to Fort Collins for a couple of weeks to rest, then headed back up to Montana with no particular plan except to visit and fish and see the country.

We'd all been worried about how Mom would handle living by herself for the first time, with her failing hearing and eyesight and intermittent respiratory problems, but I felt comforted and reassured by my visit with her. She had vehemently expressed her lack of interest in living in a retirement home. Instead she'd selected an apartment right off West 24th Street in the middle of mall sprawl and heavy traffic—

a dangerous location, as it turned out, but she could walk to do her shopping and the apartment's design and kitchen reminded her of the old Idaho home. We'd talk over coffee at her kitchen table, and then walk to breakfast places where we used to go with Dad while he gradually declined.

"You know, he never really was the way he wanted to be until this last year when he knew he was dying." Her words kept returning to me. I'd never before spent so much time just talking with her, as she wove in and out of memories about their life together. I found sharing her reflections soothing, but sometimes her stories and interpretations surprised and disconcerted me. Could his long struggle with cancer really have been the best as well as the worst of times? But her suggestion that he'd somehow become most himself while dying, in anguish and dementia, confirmed my own sense of mystery surrounding his death.

Dad had been a fallen-away Catholic who believed in reason and science and common sense pragmatism, who seemed to remain skeptical until the end about any religious or spiritual beliefs about higher powers or an afterlife. Yet there had been a new kind of grace about him in those final months, a kind of recovered innocence and peace, even as he was losing control of the very powers of mind through which he had always defined himself.

"You can just lay me out in a tree or a hillside like some of the Indians used to do," he told us once when the talk drifted toward death. "Or just cremate me. But whatever you do don't spend a fortune on an expensive damn coffin. I won't be here anyway, and as far as I'm concerned funerals are for the living, so just do whatever seems right."

My mother's words reverberated as I headed west down the Yellowstone valley to revisit my favorite fishing spots.

When I'd stopped at Dad's gravesite on my way out of town I sensed his presence there trying to comfort me. But I knew he had never believed in such things. At the age of fourteen I also turned from the church and the fear of Hell so ably instilled by those small-town Montana parishes. I'd also adopted Dad's materialist, rationalist philosophy. For me this had evolved during my college years into what I considered to be a tough-minded existentialism, a world view that survived pretty much intact until after I began teaching Native American literature and studying a Chinese Taoist martial art, Tai Chi Chuan, when I began to wonder if my skepticism wasn't just an act of faith like any other.

Sometimes I even wondered if I'd missed the point of the Catholic traditions I'd abandoned. What would Dad have to say about all this? "He never was the way he really wanted to be until he was dying," Mom had said. What could this mean?

So I fished Henry's Lake and spent some nights by the Madison River in Ennis, where Dad had spent seven years as the school superintendent. Then I decided to head north to Browning to visit my relatives and fish the Blackfeet lakes that had become my favorite fishing spots.

I'd visited the reservation for several summers in a row, ever since I'd reintroduced myself to my Blackfeet uncle Gene Ground five years earlier. My wife Liz and I had rented a room at the Warbonnet Lodge in Browning after a long afternoon traveling over the "Going to the Sun Highway" through Glacier Park, which Dad always described as the most spectacular drive in the West.

"When I was a kid we stopped in here a couple of times to visit Dad's aunt Imelda and uncle Gene," I'd told Liz. "She's passed away, but I wonder if he's still around."

When I called the number for Gene Ground in the phone book he said, "Geez, David Mogen. I haven't seen any of you kids for over twenty years. I'll be right over."

Ten minutes later he knocked on the door. I introduced him to Liz and visited about family news. When I asked about the local fly-fishing he said, "You have to try these Blackfeet lakes. Hey, I'll take you to Lost Lake out by Starr School where I grew up. I want to get some sweetgrass anyway."

An hour later I was picking up tips about local fly hatches from a Blackfeet guy fishing alongside me in his float tube when a sudden thunderstorm drove us off the lake. I slammed back into the truck dripping wet beside Gene, who'd already gathered his sweetgrass. "I'll show you how to make these braids," he said as he began wrapping the long grass. "Here, now you've got some Blackfeet sweetgrass to take home with you." And then later we met his daughter Mary Ellen and her husband Conrad out at their home by Cut Bank Creek.

Back in Fort Collins we kept the sweetgrass braids by the entryway to our home, and since then I'd come back every summer to fish and visit. I'd discovered that Mary Ellen and Conrad and I not only share common interests in Native American writing and cultural issues, but that we also share an interest in family history. And I came to realize that because her mother Imelda was my great-aunt, the youngest sister of my grandmother Frances, Mary Ellen had firsthand memories of many of Dad's older relatives whom I'd barely known. Her grandmother was my great-grandmother Lena, from that first generation of Lynches who'd arrived from Ireland in southeastern Montana back in 1883. So even though Mary Ellen was four years younger than I she was closer to that generation of pioneer Irish that I was especially curious about.

"You know your grandmother Frances didn't approve of Mom's marriage," Mary Ellen told me once when we were cleaning up after a meal of brook trout that I'd brought up from the beaver ponds down on Cut Bank Creek.

"Dad mentioned that a few times. It sounds like she tried to disown your mom or something." It had always seemed a curious and painful story to me, and I was glad she'd brought it up.

"Well, Aunt Val had Mom and Dad over to dinner with Frances and Slim at her home in Missoula, and I guess they patched it up. But I'm not sure they were ever that comfortable with each other."

She told me about how her parents had both blended their Catholic faith with their Blackfeet culture, though she, like me, had long ago rebelled against the Catholic fire and brimstone, and neither of us could really see how the doctrines we'd rejected fit with traditional Indian spirituality. When we talked about her mother's death in the hospital at Browning and her own beliefs about the afterlife, she said, "Oh, I still talk to her sometimes. And I think she's there in the Sand Hills, where Blackfeet people go when they die."

Yet Uncle Gene must somehow believe that she's in the Catholic Heaven as well, I reflected, and that those afterlife places are not as far apart as they seem. So maybe these differences in religious belief are partly a generational thing. And what if these old-timers know something we haven't figured out yet?

After drifting up to the Big Hole River I called Mary Ellen from Butte to make sure I wasn't coming at a bad time. "We were sorry to hear about your dad," she said. "We've been so busy this summer that we couldn't get away for the funeral." Since Browning is over three hundred miles from Billings and there'd only been a day's notice we hadn't expected them, but I knew being there would have been important to them. "A lot's going on," she said. "I'll explain when you get here. But come on up."

Something about that drive up to Blackfeet country always stirs things up inside me anyway, and that summer there'd been plenty of rain so the country was unusually vibrant and green. When I turned north from the interstate above Wolf Creek to drive the last 150 miles through the rolling hills and cut bank streams in that Choteau country, I felt like I was driving to the top of the world. And then there were the horse and cattle herds and the wide open land of the Blackfeet Reservation. Soon I was pulling into the driveway of their home on Cut Bank Creek with the sun going down behind the Glacier Park peaks that float above everything up there.

"Hey, you're just in time for supper," Conrad greeted me. After we ate he and Mary Ellen explained that they had to leave early in the morning because they were busy with their Medicine Lodge ceremony. Conrad had been chosen to be the Medicine Lodge man through a dream of the Medicine Woman, who was the central figure in the ceremony, so he would be fasting and praying for four days with her inside the Medicine Lodge. And tomorrow was the day when they would begin preparing over a hundred beef tongues (buffalo tongues in the old days) that the ceremony required. Conrad had packed the back of his pickup with his chainsaw and other materials to help make the Medicine Lodge.

In my previous visits I'd never suspected that they were so involved with traditional Blackfeet religious life. It wasn't until that summer that I learned that some of the rituals they observe—like never cutting meat on the grill, or leaving their door unlocked—are required because they are keepers of one of the tribe's Thunder Pipe bundles. So I got up early for breakfast feeling a bit out of place and in awe that so much that you don't know can be going on beneath the surfaces of our lives.

After breakfast Mary Ellen's manner changed abruptly.

"Before we leave there's something I want to give you," she said. She lifted a small leather pouch from her purse and placed it on the table in front of me. "This is an Iniskim, a buffalo rock. It will bring you luck. Not many from my mother's family have come to really know us, so I want to give it to you."

She slowly opened the pouch and showed me a small, red, buffalo-shaped rock inside, resting on a sweetgrass nest. She gave it to me to hold, then showed me how to rewrap it in its bundle. "Take my father out to lunch and he'll tell you the story that goes with it. And it's in my grandmother's book of stories too, the Iniskim story." The previous summer I'd bought the small book of oral tales as told by Gene's mother Mary Ground, *Grass Woman Stories*. But I'd forgotten to bring it with me, and I didn't remember the story.

When I called Uncle Gene he suggested that we drive up to East Glacier for lunch. We talked about Dad's death and family stuff. At the end of the meal I showed him the bundle that Mary Ellen had given me and explained that she'd told me to ask him to tell me the story. "Yeah, she told me about that," he said. He gazed at me thoughtfully. "I'll tell you the story on the way back."

In my memory that drive from East Glacier north to Cut Bank Creek and downstream to Conrad and Mary Ellen's home seems suspended in another dimension, as though I entered and emerged from a parallel world in which old time stories and this world we know coexist. The sun gleamed off the aspen and pine as we drove in and out of shadows cast from the gray stone peaks.

"I learned this story from my mother in Indian," Uncle Gene began. "But I'll tell it to you in English, except for the song." When he began the story his voice changed, becoming slightly higher pitched but slow and melodic, as he savored each syllable.

It was a hard winter and the people were starving, he said. *They were getting weak and sick and they were so desperate they had begun to boil their leather to make soup. The chief's youngest wife, she would go out on those cold winter mornings to gather wood for their fires. They were in country like this,* he said, waving his hand across the windshield, *camped beside a big cliff.* As I looked out the window the aspen by the road quaked in the afternoon light, and it seemed all that separated us from that camp was a ripple in time.

She was shaking those aspen branches to get the snow off when she heard this voice singing, he continued. *She kept looking and looking and finally she swept the snow off this little rock and sure enough, that rock was singing to her. "You woman over there,"* it sang. *"Take me with you. I am holy. I can help you. I want a gift. May I have a kidney to eat?"* While he sang the song in Blackfeet I felt as if inside the truck everything had become still, and we were drifting out of time and space.

She took the rock home and told the chief about it, but he scolded her and told her they were starving and didn't have time for foolishness, he continued. *But she built the rock a*

*sweetgrass nest anyway and rubbed it with a little fat and
prayed to it. And that night a blizzard came in, but when
she stepped out that morning to gather wood everything was
bright and clear, and then she noticed these large mounds beneath the cliff that hadn't been there before. And when she
brushed the snow off she found buffalo fur, and she realized
that a buffalo herd had charged over the Buffalo Jump Cliff
during the storm. They came to feed the people. So she told
the chief and the people feasted and stored meat for the rest
of the winter and she became a Medicine Woman.*

And since then, he said, *when the Blackfeet people find
these Iniskim buffalo rocks they honor them like that first Iniskim asked her to in the song. In the old days they brought
good luck in hunting buffalo, and now they bring good luck
in life.*

As I turned into the gravel driveway to my cousin's home we
seemed to have drifted back into the "real" world again. I
felt alert and attentive as Uncle Gene explained how to care
for the buffalo rock and pray with it.

"It likes being rubbed with beef fat," he explained. "Sometimes, when I need help, I just hold it in my hand and talk
to it."

As we sat there in the driveway looking south to Cut Bank
Creek he pointed out where his parents' home had been, farther west and down closer to the creek. He'd been the second
son in a row after his nine sisters were born, he explained.
"And my father, sometimes he would take me up on that
hill," he said, pointing to a rise in the bank above the creek.
"We'd sit there and he'd tell me those old stories."

We gazed out at the rolling hills winding down to the wil-
lows by the creek. I thought of Dad, and how there wasn't

much in his hardworking ranching heritage that suggested a father should take time to walk out by a river bank with his son to watch the river and tell stories.

But he did tell stories about the old times at the ranch, especially late in his life, when he realized I was interested in those things. And those were some of the best times, when he and Mom and aunts and uncles and their friends would tell their stories about the old days. Though they often told of tough times and hardship, like the Iniskim story, they brought the past to life with vitality and strong humor.

I got out late that afternoon because I couldn't leave the beaver ponds down on Cut Bank Creek. The brook trout eagerly slammed big attracter dry flies, their jeweled bodies sparkling in the sun and the cold, crystal water. I'd learned to move carefully in the treacherous silt mud after slipping into a sinkhole and ripping my waders. And Mary Ellen had warned me about fishing there until dark and coming up the riverbank with fresh trout, since they'd had reports of a grizzly roaming the creek. But I always looked forward to finishing my trip battling those wild trout down by the willow banks. And that afternoon they seemed charged with energy from the recent storm, surging back to the banks as I released them from the big caddis and grasshopper patterns.

I kept some trout to leave with Mary Ellen and Conrad, and saved several more for breakfast with Mom the next morning. I called from Great Falls a few hours down the road to tell her I'd be getting in late, which she seemed to expect. She was up reading when I finally arrived at one in the morning. "Oh, they're so beautiful," she said when I displayed the brilliantly colored brook trout in her kitchen sink.

"I've got something to show you, Mom," I said. "This is

probably the most unexpected gift I've ever received. It means a lot to me, but I'm not sure I understand what receiving it means." I displayed the bundle, then opened it and handed her the Iniskim. She stroked the little stone in her hand.

"I've always wondered what might be inside one of these Indian pouches," she said. "Why it looks like a little buffalo, but it hasn't been carved." So I told her how I'd come to receive the bundle and the story of its origin, how people just find buffalo rocks up there in Blackfeet country like the Iniskim story says. Discussion about prayer objects was an unusual topic for us. I suspect I had always seemed to share my father's view that such things are essentially foolish.

"You know, when your brother Mike went to Italy I asked him to get me some of those rosaries blessed by the Pope," she said, abruptly gliding to the closet to return with a little bag containing two small boxes. She displayed the rosaries then handed them to me. "One is for Mabel," she continued, referring to my dad's youngest sister, who also lives in Billings.

She looked at me speculatively while I felt the texture of the beads. "I've always wanted one of these in my hand when I'm buried, in the old Catholic way." She seemed almost shy. "Like this," she showed me, draping the rosary around her hand in front of her heart.

I was surprised and touched. She hadn't attended Mass regularly since we were kids. But by now I'd begun to realize the power that these old stories possess, as they play out beneath the surface of our lives. And when Mom unexpectedly died two years from that Christmas I told the family about our conversation. Now I remember Mom in her coffin in her favorite rose-colored dress with her rosary clasped above her heart.

As I drifted off to sleep that night I imagined an encounter between a young Cheyenne woman and one of those Lynch girls from that first generation, whose original homestead, until 1897, was on what is now the Cheyenne reservation. Perhaps she was my great-grandmother Lena, who spoke Cheyenne but was raised in the Old World Catholicism her family had brought from Ireland. I imagine her giving an old cherished crucifix and a rosary to her Cheyenne friend and explaining the story they represent. How the Great Spirit's son chose to be born in human form to be sacrificed on the cross to bring a story of love and healing. And how when they performed the Mass at nearby St. Labre mission they recreated the story of his last supper, when the ordinary bread and wine transforms into his flesh and blood.

As I imagined this conversation I felt for the first time the potential healing energy of the stories embodied in that old cross and string of beads. Like the story embodied in this little stone, I thought, and for the first time I understood how an Indian elder like my uncle Gene could blend his Blackfeet medicine with his Catholic faith. I don't know what powers these objects might have beyond what can be explained by pure reason and science and common sense, but I know that they carry the power of these stories that can grace and transform our lives.

And of course there are all the stories of conflict, and the truths they carry as well. Like the story of Lena's daughter Imelda, who settled in Browning to become part of the Blackfeet people, and her estrangement from her oldest sister, Frances, my grandmother, whose memory I also honor. And there's the long history of violence and oppression and misunderstanding, much of it still unresolved, woven into the frontier story in which all these ancestors played a part.

But woven alongside those stories of conflict, like the strands of the sweetgrass braids I received from my uncle Gene, are these other stories that have not been told enough, stories about people who have shared medicine across imagined frontier lines, who have helped each other to heal old, festering wounds.

So I returned home from northern Montana that summer with a leather bundle that I know I will never understand entirely. But I also know that the powers of such things are to be felt rather than merely explained. "It's a gift given to you," Mary Ellen said the following summer, when I explained my apprehension that I would leave Iniskim untouched simply because I feared using it foolishly or inappropriately. "Just pay attention and listen."

Sometimes when I hold this buffalo rock, especially when I'm trying to figure out something important, I feel it vibrate with its song at some subsonic stone frequency that I can feel but not hear. And I wonder—I don't really believe such things, but I no longer disbelieve them either—I wonder if my father somehow hears it singing as well, with my mother by his side stroking her rosary, in the midst of mysteries he no longer struggles to explain.

Searching for Marcus Daly

What then is the American, this new man? . . . Here individuals of all nations are melted into a new race of men, whose labours and posterity will one day cause great changes in the world. Americans are the western pilgrims, who are carrying along with them that great mass of arts, sciences, vigour, and industry which began long since in the east; they will finish the great circle.

—JEAN DE CREVECOEUR, "What is an American?"
in *Letters from an American Farmer*, 1782

I can tell by your outfit that you are a cowboy.

—"Streets of Laredo"

I'm looking for a book called *The War of the Copper Kings* on the shelves of Montana writings in the small but beautifully stocked Blue Heron bookstore in Ennis, where I've stopped on my first Montana fly-fishing trip of the summer. I've decided to find out more about Marcus Daly, one of the Butte "Copper Kings," partly out of idle curiosity and partly because he's linked to the family history I've been exploring. He and his cousin, my great-great-granduncle Jack Lynch, grew up on neighboring farms in Ireland. Jack, who somehow ended up in partnership with Daly on a cattle ranch in southeastern Montana, convinced my great-great-grandparents Patrick and Margaret Lynch to leave the misery of colonized Ireland and join him on the newly opened Montana frontier, where a hometown boy like Marcus Daly could become fabulously rich and powerful, and where pretty much everybody of European descent seemed to be doing okay.

Now I'm curious about the Butte big money connection to my southeastern Montana ranching heritage, which I'd always imagined consisted of working cowboys settled into homesteads and family ranches. Until recently I'd never imagined a connection between them and the most notorious of the "Copper Kings," who essentially ran Montana politics at the end of the nineteenth-century.

When I visited my friend Bill Macgregor, who taught at the Montana School of Mines in Butte, I encountered the statue of Marcus Daly at the entrance to campus. He stands on a pedestal with his coat draped across his left arm, hat in hand. I imagined him recently arrived from the mining frontiers of California and Nevada, surveying what was then just mining shacks scattered across a mountainside but is now the city of Butte, sprawled beneath the huge open pit mine down into the valley below.

Something about his posture reminded me of my own memory of standing, suitcases in hand, transfixed by my first view of the Columbia University campus. This was his new world, as Manhattan was mine, though of course he went on to become a powerful multi-millionaire instead of just a kid with a college degree. Curious as the connection seemed, I resolved to find out more about him. I have this vague suspicion that without Marcus Daly I wouldn't be here.

The only copy of *Copper Kings* is an expensive first edition, so I select a more economical contemporary history, Michael P. Malone's *The Battle of Butte*, after I pause thoughtfully over his early description of Marcus Daly as "a hearty and likable man who never pretended to be anything more than he really was, a working miner who made it big," whose "unaffected simplicity made him a popular favorite in the democratic, hairy-chested mining camp of Butte."

I browse through the rest of the extensive collection, surprised at the sheer volume of writing about Montana, almost as amazed as I am to discover such a sophisticated collection and bookstore owner here in Ennis. I've just wandered over after a cheeseburger and a piece of pie at the Ennis Café across the street, where my sister Doris worked as a waitress during her summers in college back when it was Herb and Wilma's Café.

I've been thumbing through *Doc*, a local autobiography on display, remembering my mother's admiration for old Doc Losee during her years working as a nurse at the small local hospital. I'm pleased to discover that her old boss is a good storyteller who, as a doctor, puts an original spin on the familiar story of settling in the West.

I was a bit surprised that the older guy in the fly store down the street didn't remember my father, but then I realized that he's probably as new to the town as some of these fancy fly stores and restaurants. It's been almost thirty years since Dad was superintendent of the school that looks down on Main Street from the hill at the west end of town. He actually steered through the bond bill that financed the new building that—along with his fondness for arguments in bars, somehow inflamed by his return to ranching country—helped cost him his job a few years later.

Ennis was still a cowboy town back then, before the Madison River became an international fishing Mecca, before the new yuppie "Old West style" businesses filled every available space along the road through town, before the Grizzly

Bar forty miles upriver expanded from serving cheeseburgers and huge t-bones and beer to a new menu and wine list
and décor that seem to have come straight from northern
California.

But I actually like the variety and the bookstore, I reflect,
finding myself on the verge of a curmudgeonly lament for
good old days that were in many ways a pain in the ass. I
had more than one confrontation in the Silver Dollar Saloon
during the summer after I graduated from Columbia when
I worked here on a construction job, still wearing my aca-
demic-hippy long hair and beard, lacking the good sense—
just like Dad—to stay out of bars and away from arguments
about the Vietnam War.

Dad was my original flawed western hero, I've come to realize. Like all of us kids, I loved and admired him. But he
broke our hearts.

"I grew up trying to be like him," I explained to Liz after our first family reunion together. "But since I left home
it seems like I've been trying to figure out how not to be like
him, how to find a new way."

Boom and bust. Mostly Dad was booming while I was
growing up, but he suddenly went bust after I left. For reasons none of us ever really understood, he quit his job in
Froid when a couple of his critics got elected to the school
board. Then he moved the family to Plentywood, where he
tried to make a living selling insurance, a job for which he
was temperamentally unfit since he had no ability to com-
promise his version of truth to close a sale. When I returned
home for Christmas after my sophomore year I was stunned
to see that he seemed to have aged twenty years. My forceful,
witty hero shuffled around, looking lost and confused.

The following year he took the job as superintendent here in Ennis in the most beautiful valley in the world, and for a few years he recaptured his old magic. He passed a bond and built a new school, making big changes as was his pattern. But in the process he acquired enemies, which was also his pattern, and this time he responded by drinking himself out of the job.

Something about being back in cowboy country triggered his response, I suspect, as though he were trying to resolve his ambivalence about his old ranching culture by swapping drinks in the bars. But I'll never really know. That was part of the cowboy code. Tough it out. Cowboy up. Just ignore contradictions, in your code and in yourself.

Boom and bust. After Ennis he had some good years in Belfry, over by the Beartooth Mountains, but there he got fired over a dispute with a school board about what he considered to be micromanaging the school. For similar reasons in mid-year he quit his last job in Savage, back up in northeastern Montana, and retired to Idaho. He became a crazy, distraught drunk for several years, and then he just quit drinking, except for an occasional beer. He never talked about it, never went for professional help. He just quit. We all toughed it out with him through the bad times, and waited for things to get better. And they always did, in the end.

He made a lot of changes to get from where he started to where he ended up, but it never was an easy ride. He knew to get back in the saddle after he was thrown, but the broncos he rode never seemed to stay broke.

All of these reflections in the Ennis bookstore might be my way of internally establishing my credentials as a true Montanan, I suppose—something that had never occurred to me until recently as either complicated or necessary. But being a Montanan apparently isn't as simple as it used to be. Defining who is and isn't an "authentic" Montanan has become a contentious issue in some of the books I'm browsing through.

Where I grew up, in small towns across the Montana Hi-Line, no one concerned themselves much with defining Montana identity. There were lots of stories about the old ranching and farming days when older folks got together, especially at holidays. But they were as much about the Old West as anything specific to Montana. Then, of course, there were North Dakota jokes:

> Q: What happened when the North Dakotan threw a grenade across the border?
>
> A: The Montanan pulled out the pin and threw it back.

Which always struck me as delightfully absurd, especially when I was going to high school in Froid. Eastern Montana, western North Dakota. Same country, same people. But because we were thirty miles west of this imaginary line we could lob these jokes at the folks on the other side. Identity jokes as cultural weaponry. Shortly after we married I decided to share my hilarity with Liz, whose father is from North Dakota. But she just got this pained look after my first few North Dakota jokes, so, in the interests of preserving marital harmony, I stopped.

Surveying this impressive array of books about Montana brings up a subject I've been thinking about a lot after Dad's death—contemplating my identity both as a westerner and, more specifically, as a Montanan. I left the Hi-Line for college at the age of eighteen, and I recently realized that I've lived in Colorado longer than I lived in Montana. So am I now a Coloradoan, rather than a Montanan? Can I be both? And a westerner too, and an American, and a citizen of the world and the universe as well?

I seem to be searching for some kind of personal and family origin story in Montana, because that's where my family's from in ways that seem important to me though their significance is sometimes elusive. That search has taken me to Ireland and could take me to Norway and Germany as well, to discover more about the origins of ancestors whose stories all converge in those early frontier days in Montana. And sometimes I think that I should just fish the rivers and enjoy the changing scenery, and not bother to find out more about Marcus Daly and the web of stories and ancestors that partially shape who I am.

In her memoir, *Through the Rosebuds* (1987), my great-aunt Margaret Broadus Bailey, daughter of Alice Lynch of that first generation of pioneers, recounts the origin story of my Irish ranching ancestors—including, I was surprised to discover, Marcus Daly. She begins her story by etching in the desperation of the Irish in the Old World, where after centuries of being defined as savages by the British, they survived in wretched misery: "Life in British-dominated Ireland was nearly intolerable, with extremely poor economic conditions, unrealistically small farms of low productivity, and many restrictive laws that discriminated against Roman Catholics. There was very little chance of anyone other than those of British descent or the Protestant faith to own property or improve their conditions. Starvation was a very common cause of death."

The exodus to the New World had already begun before her grandparents, Patrick and Margaret Lynch, joined the quest for a new beginning. "Years before she [Alice Lynch] was born, many members of both the Lynch and Callan families had already begun immigrating to America to escape from poverty and the dismal conditions in their homeland. Patrick and Margaret longed to join their adventurous relatives, but stayed behind to care for Patrick's aging mother."

When they finally escaped these bogs of tradition and despair after Patrick's mother died, they first joined other relatives in Illinois. But from there they were indirectly drawn to the Montana frontier by their cousin Marcus Daly, who grew up "in Derrylea near Ballyjamesduff . . . across the lane from the Lynch family farm."

My great-aunt's account emphasizes the central role that Jack Lynch and Marcus Daly played in luring our ancestors to the western frontier:

> The Lynches stayed in Illinois for several months but letters kept coming from the West, telling of wonderful opportunities in Montana Territory. . . . At the time, an uncle, Jack Lynch, was operating a cattle ranch at the mouth of Lame Deer Creek along the Rosebud . . . in a partnership arrangement with his cousin, Marcus Daly of Butte, who later became known as one of Montana's great "Copper Kings." He maintained contact with his former neighbors and helped them where he could with a job or a grubstake as he built an empire in the copper industry. . . . Accepting Jack Lynch's invitation to join him in Montana, my grandparents . . . packed up and headed west over the new Northern Pacific Railroad. They arrived at the town of Rosebud in October of 1883, with all of their possessions.

To be honest, until I encountered this family history I would never have conceived of Marcus Daly as an authentic western hero, since as a rich miner he seemed disqualified for the role both by class and profession. Yet after reading accounts of his life and participation in the Copper Wars in Butte— the Irish king battling for control of the new state government with his Scots-Irish rival, William A. Clark—I grudgingly admitted that he plays an intriguing and in some ways admirable part in the family saga. Given his circumstances he made the most of his opportunities through an impressive combination of pluck, luck, and applied intelligence. And whatever I might think of his big-money politics, without his influence my dad's Irish ancestors might never have arrived in Montana.

Besides creating his own rags-to-riches story, Marcus Daly displayed determination to help friends and family benefit from his success. In *The Battle of Butte* Malone depicts Daly as a ruthless frontier capitalist titan who also took care of his own people: "He was a man of the earth, whose stocky frame, stooping shoulders, brusque mannerisms, simple tastes, and open and unpretentious personality all bore evidence of his Irish peasant roots."

In defining Daly's legacy Malone emphasizes that family and friends, as opposed to enemies, remembered him as a powerful, protective "father-figure":

> Marcus Daly was a man to remember, a Horatio Alger hero who had fought his way from dire poverty to fabulous riches, a true empire builder. He was a man of polar extremes in his character: as Clark's *Butte Miner* put it, "a friend to his friends, to his enemies bitter, remorseless, and unforgiving." Seen at his best, Daly the father-figure watched over his family, his friends, and employees with a genuine, heartfelt benevolence; and history must also note that, so long as he ran

the Anaconda, it treated its employees better than most cor-
porations of the time. At his worst, he was ruthless, vindic-
tive, and tyrannical. Like the mining frontier that molded
him, he was rough-hewn and unlettered, yet also sentimental, decent, and generous. His legacy seems as polarized as
his character.

To my Lynch ancestors arriving by railroad to begin their
new life as Montana ranchers, Marcus Daly was most em-
phatically family. He celebrated their new beginning by starting their cattle herd.

I learned about this gift at the June 2009 Lynch-Callan
Reunion, where over two hundred descendants of Patrick
and Margaret Lynch received booklets filled with old photos and family history, in which family historian Cathy Byron sketches in more detail about the family origin story. It
turns out that the family connection to Marcus Daly was
more intimate than I had imagined, since Daly's gift of cattle
was payment for a loan that helped launch his original journey to America: "Mary Lynch Mahoney [the oldest Lynch
daughter] told her children that PHL [Patrick Hugh Lynch]
loaned Marcus money when he left to seek his fortune in
America, and that Marcus repaid that loan by having cattle
waiting for him when he arrived in Montana."

I'm particularly intrigued by Byron's interpretation of the
role played by Patrick's younger brother Jack, the original
Irish cowboy in this saga. Byron observes that his "colorful
legacy is carried down the family line through a rich oral legacy recalling, and embellishing, his many antics. . . . Jack met
the Patrick Hugh Lynch and Ellen Lynch Gaffney families
with three teams and wagons when they got off the train in
Rosebud in October 1883. The 'four old ones and fourteen

young uns' spent the winter at Jack's cowboy camp waiting for the spring."

So now any romantic constructions of my western heritage have to accommodate not only honyockers, who plowed the earth, but an oligarch who helped transform mountains into toxic sludge.

Reflecting on all the complications of this American and western, and now Montanan, preoccupation with defining roots and authenticity, I sometimes wonder if a Native American colleague of mine was right when he observed that there is no such thing as American identity. "But good Lord," I responded, "the library is filled with books about American identity. Some of my colleagues and I have even written some of them."

And then it occurred to me that perhaps this ongoing search for identity and roots does reveal a truth at the center of discussions of American character, and a core truth within all these regional mythologies that spin off from it. What if our ongoing identity crisis profoundly defines our national character? What if the unique feature of American identity is that it can't be defined? What if we are the one nation on earth that has no recognizable identity, which is precisely why we've devoted so much energy to answering Crevecoeur's unanswerable question: What is an "American"? And now we grapple with these other identity issues that flow from it. What is a "westerner"? What is a "Montanan"? What is a "honyocker"?

Maybe we're obsessed with what we don't have, and still seek to shape an origin story to tell us who we are and why we're here and how to live in harmony with this land. And perhaps the absence of a coherent story that's sufficiently flex-

ible to embrace all of our diversity actually perpetuates the vexed freedom we cherish so highly, haunted as we are by the refrain of that eloquent statement about American identity, "Me and Bobby McGee," which suggests that "freedom" is just our chosen name "for nothing left to lose."

Or perhaps we only imagine that more traditional cultures provide simpler and clearer models for identity. Maybe some of the issues are just different. In fact I wonder if establishing identity in traditional cultures is more complex, especially since today most tribal people have to integrate identities from both worlds.

Conversations with my Blackfeet relatives in recent years have complicated my vision of preserving tribal identity. My late uncle Gene Ground was an elder Blackfeet speaker who in many ways embodied tribal traditions, but he was also a devout Catholic who loved his veterans' meetings in Great Falls.

Perhaps witnessing my cousin Mary Ellen and her husband Conrad prepare for their annual Medicine Lodge ceremony the previous summer helped inspire these reflections. There's the physical work they do, such as building the Medicine Lodge and preparing the beef tongues, in addition to the years they spent learning and maintaining the ceremonies themselves. And meanwhile they both work at their professional jobs in tribal offices in Browning. Preserving tradition can be hard work, especially when you have a full-time day job on the side.

Over the years I've also realized that my conversations with Mary Ellen have provided me with a valuable perspective on my own Irish heritage. That summer after my father died from cancer, while we were doing dishes after our annual feast of brook trout caught in the beaver dams on Cut

Bank Creek behind their home, I asked Mary Ellen about the death of her mother, Dad's aunt Imelda. A strong, nurturing woman whom I remembered fondly from visiting with her as a kid while Uncle Gene went to school on the G.I. Bill in Missoula, she worked as an RN at the tribal hospital for decades and knew pretty much everyone in the tribe. Mary Ellen said she stopped taking medication when she knew it was time, and people filed in for days to say goodbye to her on her death bed.

"And there's one thing she told me when I was a girl that I'll never forget," Mary Ellen said, turning from the sink to look me in the eye. "She said, always be proud of being Blackfeet. But don't ever forget that you're part Irish, too." We'd talked about our own bitter experiences with the Catholic Church, but she told me that her mother's faith always seemed different from the grim doctrine that was terrorized into us in catechism class. Her mother listened for the banshee, she said, and her old Irish Catholicism never seemed inconsistent with belief in Blackfeet spirits.

And it was through Mary Ellen that I got some sense of what the family connection to Marcus Daly meant to my grandmother's generation. "When we'd get together with Aunt Val in Great Falls, or anyone in Mom's family, someone would bring up Marcus Daly and wonder if somehow we might not get just a bit of that inheritance." She chuckled at the memory. "We spent my whole childhood waiting for that Daly money to appear, but he never did come through."

At the time, I decided that that whimsical summary best defined the family relationship to our most legendary Irish relative. I originally intended the story title, "Searching for Marcus Daly," to parallel "Waiting for Godot," suggesting an ending both anti-climactic and absurd. Marcus Daly rep-

resented only a fanciful connection to power, I'd concluded, while family frontier heroes like Patrick and Margaret Lynch and Grandpa Slim and Great-Aunt Imelda had come to life in my imagination as emblems of our true ranching legacy.

But now that I know more about the family origin story, my search has an ending after all. I no longer see Marcus Daly as just a statue. I can now visualize the driven, ambitious Irish kid who became the impressive but static monument. He's a vivid character in the family legacy, who dramatizes contradictions in our pioneer heritage. And perhaps "inheritance" in this kind of story includes things such as drive and character, and cannot be measured simply by cattle and money after all.

In the spring of 2008 I finally arrived at the sites of the old Lynch and Daly farms in Ireland. For years I'd nursed a vague ambition to visit these origin places, and after I accepted a faculty residence position at Swansea University in Wales that spring, I finally sought them out. Liz and I drove from Sligo up through Northern Ireland and back down, just across the border to the town of Cavan, where we spent a night at a historic downtown hotel drinking Guinness and listening to traditional Irish music in the pub. At the genealogy office of the County Cavan library the next morning we met with Mary Sullivan. She actually owns a copy of Margaret Broadus Bailey's *Through the Rosebuds*, and on the basis of the book's descriptions we managed to locate the old Lynch and Daly farms on an area map.

We threaded our way through the narrow Irish roads to the village of Ballyjamesduff, where we consulted with a fellow at the local museum whom Mary Sullivan had notified about our mission. After some phone calls he gave us precise information about how to locate the crossing. So finally late in the afternoon, we found the old stone building that remains of the Daly place, and the farmyard across the road, now filled with farm equipment, where Patrick Lynch grew up. I leaned over to pick something up from the rocky soil.

"What is it?" asked Liz.

I showed her the small gray stone, polished it with my handkerchief, and then placed it in my pocket. "It's the Lynch Stone of Cavan," I explained.

Nothing was as I'd imagined it. For some reason I'd always assumed that the farming country of County Cavan would be similar to that of northeastern Montana, just with smaller farms and more people. I knew that when the Lynches left they'd been desperately poor, and that their farm wasn't large enough to support them. But things have obviously changed. Cavan County today seems both prosperous and crowded. The land may be stony but it's lush and green, and the county road on which the old farms are located is so densely populated with modern homes that it seems like a suburban street.

We drove several miles through the countryside to find the family church in the middle of Lynch and Callan country. Off the main county road the farmhouses were more dispersed, more like the countryside I'd imagined, and when we found the entrance we drove up the driveway, expecting to find a modest country chapel. We encountered the graveyard first, two expansive fields crowded with gravestones, many of them several feet in height. From our pathway I scanned them, noticing several large groups of Lynches and another of Callans. At the top of the hill loomed Crosserlough Church.

"Good Lord, it's practically a cathedral," I observed to Liz as we opened the large wooden door. We were the only ones there on a quiet Monday afternoon. We had toured much larger and more famous cathedrals during our previous travels in Europe, but we had never encountered one so unexpectedly, where we were free to wander through it completely on our own. We marveled at the spaciousness, the intricate stained glass Stations of the Cross, in such a quiet country setting.

"And this is his chapel," I whispered.

As we prepared to leave we had stopped in a back corner to observe the large, dramatic crucifix at the center of the Marcus Daly Chapel, built by Daly in 1895 in honor of his mother, the commemorative plaque explains. I suspect that the monumental size of the church itself was inspired by Marcus Daly money.

All of that copper ore torn from the richest hill on earth back in the Rockies, I thought, to shape this tribute to his mother, faith, and newly minted wealth, here in this Irish countryside where generations of our ancestors are buried. Like Daly himself, perhaps, the church is a bit extravagant for its setting, but it's a symbol of Daly's connection to his Irish Catholic roots and his pride in his family and heritage, even at the height of his power in the new American oligarchy.

So where does Marcus Daly fit into the family legacy?

As I survey my growing pantheon of family frontier figures I realize that some fascinate me because they embody familiar archetypes of the West, others because they disrupt them, and most because they do both.

Patrick and Margaret Lynch are the immigrant pioneer ancestors, lured to a distant wilderness by the promise of a fresh start, populating their new land with generations to come. But that archetype is complicated precisely by their relationship with Marcus Daly, their fabulously rich cousin who sent them a gift of cattle as his greeting to the Montana frontier.

Grandpa Slim rides into my imagination straight from the pages of *The Virginian*, an orphan kid growing into manhood in the early cowboy frontier, though he would have been the first Norwegian cowboy in Wister's Anglo-centric vision.

And Great-Aunt Imelda fascinates me because she rebelled against her pioneer tradition. At a time when it was a rare and almost unthinkable option for a white woman, she chose to marry into a Native tribe and to raise her family on a reservation. She faced the shocked disapproval of her older sister and conventional opinion, and became a healing figure among her new Blackfeet people. Yet in a paradoxical sense that perhaps makes her the most archetypal pioneer of them all, since she so dramatically left her Old World behind to make a new life.

Perhaps my confusion about how to integrate Marcus Daly into the family origin story comes down to one thing. He was rich. And this is where I realize I'm testing the meanings of an identity I'm partially shaping as a write. What, after all, is a "honyocker"? If I've stretched the original meanings of "honyocker" to include not just immigrant farmers but also the small ranchers and cowboys from my dad's family (a "stretcher" they might not accept), where does this wealthy and powerful family oligarch fit in? On some level I've transformed the old insult, "honyocker," into a rough, humorous ideal of working class roots. Can a rich miner enter into this honyocker world?

If not, perhaps even my own expansive definition has become too rigid. I remember contemplating the small stone buildings across what was just a country lane in Old Ireland when Marcus Daly and Jack Lynch were boys. They started together here, I thought, working and playing on their hardscrabble land like so many of my Montana pioneer ancestors.

Marcus Daly left for the New World at the age of fifteen with a small loan from his cousin Patrick Lynch, learned the mining trade from the bottom up, and fought his way to wealth and power in tough times, succeeding through intense application of his untutored intelligence and the sheer force of his vision and will. He never forgot or ignored his working class origins. If rebelling against pioneer tradition makes Great-Aunt Imelda the most archetypal of pioneers, perhaps, while ripping wealth and status from his new land yet never abandoning his connections to his Old World roots, Marcus Daly became the ultimate honyocker.

Honyocker dreams, indeed—busted dreams, booming dreams, some shattered or fulfilled beyond measure. Where do they begin? Where do they end?

Beside the Stillwater

The Tao that can be spoken is not the true Tao.

—TAO TE CHING

And while I stood there I saw more than I can tell and I understood more than I saw . . .

—*Black Elk Speaks*

It's two in the morning and I can't sleep. It's slipping away. Something I felt on the trail as I looked down from the steep bank of the west fork of the Stillwater River into water so clear that it etches the color and shape of each stone. Vivid clarity, yet shimmering from the water's motion so that the precise shapes seem portals to another world. Lucidity sharpened through the lens of moving water. Stillness I had never experienced so deeply, yet motion and change, there in the jeweled streambed and crystal water. Already slipping away.

Yesterday morning I woke up on my fifth day alone in the wilderness, and I finally knew I was going to make it back out, wondering if my lingering sense of peril had been there all along to heighten the drama of whatever story I was enacting. This was one of those dream-come-true kind of stories, I'd decided, in which you learn to be careful of what you wish for.

It all happened so quickly, so unexpectedly. I'd arrived in Billings for the annual backpack trip into the Beartooths with my youngest brother, Kirk. It had begun like all our trips, although this time we were accompanied by his wife, Jill, and his teenage stepdaughter, Christina. As always we were late getting packed, late to the trail, and slowed this time by my last-minute decision in Absarokee to buy dry flies and new backpacking wading boots, by highway construction, by rocky roads to the trailhead that could not be rushed.

At 2:30 in the heat of the day we finally started up the trail on a route that had never quite made sense to me. "Twelve miles," Kirk had said initially, a week earlier, when I'd passed through on my way to a week of fishing up by Glacier Park. "But it's easy trail, except for the last few miles, and then we'll be at Wounded Man Lake. You can day-hike to Lake Martee, with the biggest cutthroats in the Beartooths, and it's only five miles across the plateau to Lightning Lake, the best lake for purebreed Goldens in the country."

Which sounded irresistible, especially the parts about the cutthroats and Goldens, but my mind informed by memory kept making uncomfortable calculations. *Only* five miles to Lightning Lake? That's ten miles of bushwhacking, even if it is plateau—all hiking and no fishing. Twelve *miles* before there's any fishing at all? Two *days* before I even get a line into the water? But by the time I'd finished a satisfying week of fishing for big trout on the Blackfeet Reservation I'd decided with some misgivings to go along.

I usually only do this once a year, and with all my fishing gear I carry a heavy pack, so warning lights in my mind kept going off, reminding me of what an ordeal it actually can be, especially when you're not in particularly good shape, to carry a pack up those mountain trails. But we had six days, and Kirk insisted it was mostly easy trail.

"It's fifteen miles to Wounded Man Lake," Jill said on the

phone when I told her I was driving across Montana from East Glacier to meet up with them.

"Fifteen? Kirk said it was twelve."

"Fifteen," she had replied. And three or four miles up the trail, when we were all pulling hard in the heat and complaining about how heavy our packs were, she said, "You know, the sign at the trailhead said it was seventeen miles to Wounded Man Lake."

"What is it about this place?" I muttered. "The harder I try to get there the farther away it gets." It was late afternoon and we were wearing out and had run out of water. We still had twelve miles to go, including the final climb above tree line, when we finally found a decent camping spot in a meadow just a few miles short of Breakneck Park Meadow, our original goal. I was exhausted, but actually holding up pretty well it seemed since Kirk, who usually pulled out ahead of everyone, caved in sooner than I did.

"I'm not going to make it," Kirk told me despondently the next morning. "My hip's killing me. It held up fine on day-hikes, but carrying the pack has really messed it up." He was limping around the campsite, obviously hurting. He'd told me about his hip earlier in the summer but had seemed confident that it was back to normal. Neither of us had any premonition then that he was suffering from a congenital condition that would ultimately require hip-replacement surgery.

"If you're not going to make it, better to bail sooner than later," I said, shocked into concern, disappointment, and relief at the sudden prospect of avoiding the long trail ahead. So we talked glumly about alternative plans for car-camping and day-hiking, while drinking instant espresso and munching on breakfast.

I tried to make Kirk feel better while grappling with my own frustration at the thought of hiking for two days, carrying the packs up and down the trail without ever seeing high country scenery, without getting a chance to test my new four-weight three-piece Winston rod on those brilliant high mountain Beartooth trout. I thought that was what drew me back every year, the spectacular fishing for vivid brook trout and cutthroats and rainbows and, on Sylvan Lake a few years back, the Golden trout, hybrid exotics of the Beartooths.

Now that my initial relief at avoiding the grueling hike had faded, I was consumed with visions of splendors ahead I would never see. My mind began composing an elegy for my lost trip up the Stillwater. All this slogging up the river trail, never to see Wounded Man Lake, or the headwaters of the west fork of the Stillwater, or the cutthroats of Lake Martee . . .

Then the revelation hit, as I was setting up my pack for our return. I'd always fantasized about doing a solitary mountain hike, a kind of improvised backpacker's vision quest. My pack's set up, I realized, and I've got a clear trail laid out. I've done this enough with more experienced trail-savvy companions that maybe now I can make it on my own. Five days and four nights in the wilderness by myself.

"Well, you'd need the water pump," Kirk said when I described my increasingly compelling idea to him. "And the bear rope. But if anything happens, like a sprained ankle even . . . you'll be a long way out, with no way to contact anybody. Be careful."

I decided to survive on dry food to avoid the bother of cooking, and because it seemed more consistent with my notions of Indian warriors and mountain men living on dried meat and pemmican. So I loaded up on granola bars, two large blocks of cheddar cheese, a couple of bags of nuts, and a substantial summer sausage. After Kirk reviewed with me how to use them, I threw the water pump and bear rope in my pack and started up the trail. It was already late morning, and I wondered if I really could make twelve miles by the end of the day, but I knew I had to get moving or give up my sudden chance to fulfill what I had assumed to be an idle dream.

"Good God, I'm actually doing it," I thought, at once excited and apprehensive. A vague fantasy I'd never even visualized clearly was becoming real with each step. Kirk's young dog Merlin suddenly appeared by my side a quarter mile up the trail, assuming with perfect canine logic that I was just out ahead of the pack. I had to drive him away, yelling, "Go," even throwing a stone in his direction until, surprised and confused, he finally lit out back down the trail. I watched him disappear around the bend, my last companion chased away.

And then I'm moving up the trail, gaining confidence with each stride, thinking, I've still got a lot of daylight left. At least I'm starting earlier than we did yesterday. This is a relatively easy trail, as Kirk said, though I'm also remembering a fuller version of his memory from last night. "Geez, it's longer and tougher than I remembered. Of course I was in the best shape I've ever been in back then, carrying a lighter pack, trying to keep up with this woman friend who was a backpacking Amazon." Great, I'm thinking. So this whole trip is based on distorted memories of some youthful time with energy to burn that neither of us will ever see again.

A couple coming down the trail pause for water and conversation and the usual exchange of information between backpackers entering and leaving.

"Where're you coming from?" I ask.

"Nine miles upriver, at the headwaters. We were at Wounded Man Lake the night before."

"Fishing any good?"

"Okay. Nothing great. How far are you going?"

"I'm hoping to get to Wounded Man tonight."

The man looks at his watch. "No way. You'll be lucky to get to the headwaters tonight, going uphill."

"Oh, I don't know," the woman reflects. "If you really push you might make it." They're both superbly fit, and they have that faraway look in their eyes that I've noticed in some backpackers on their way out of the wild.

"Good luck," she says. Her eyes flash cobalt blue. "We're looking forward to eating a steak and sleeping in a bed. It's beautiful though. Have a good trip."

So I stride into Breakneck Park Meadow an hour later, feeling the rhythm of the trail, still sorting out whether I feel foreboding or reassurance from my earlier encounter. Where the river turns south Breakneck Park Meadow opens out from the forest in a broad sweeping curve, a spot so beautiful and open that it's been somewhat developed as a camping center for horse-outfitters, with a small shed and a horse shelter at the west edge of the meadow.

A young cowboy in a black hat stands by the trail at the edge of the river, where I set down my pack for a lunch break. We're watching a man cast his fly line downstream in the sparkling river, without leaving slack for drift, while kids splash in the water beside him.

"That's a technique I haven't seen before," I observe. I

can't tell whether he's actually trying to get a natural drift on the fly, has no idea what he's doing, or is just idly playing around.

"There's no fish in here anyway," says the cowboy. "A bunch that was in here before us fished this section out. It'll be days before they're back in here again." He's obviously used to shepherding tourists in and out, disgusted with the group that cleaned out all the trout.

"You all alone?" he asks, so I explain about my brother's injury and my decision to wing it alone. We're watching the man cast while I eat lunch, and when I tell him I teach at Colorado State he explains that though he lives on a nearby ranch he's from a University of Wyoming family, and he's just finished his junior year playing football there.

"You stole that game from us last year on our home field," I observe. The sun is warm and the meadow peaceful and we both watch the river flow as we weave into and out of stories.

Finally I look at my watch, stand up, and swing my backpack up on my back. He looks me in the eye and grins. "Hey, have a good trip. You'll run into more groups on horseback going up the trail. Not many backpackers though. Most people don't want to carry their packs that far."

Which reminds me that I've just started on a trail that will take me thirty-four miles by the time I'm done, and I've probably just had my last extended conversation with anyone for days. So I start the last nine miles up to Wounded Man Lake wondering whether I should just kick back at the meadow instead, and watch the river flow.

But now I'm pushing up the trail through thick forest. I'd assumed from my map that I'd be hiking beside the river, with comfortable campsites pretty much everywhere, but that's the problem with maps, especially when you're an amateur at reading them. They can't tell you what the country's really like.

The river actually gurgles down below me in heavy brush, the mosquitoes and deerflies dance around me, and the area seems to specialize in that most spectacular of insect assailants, the horse fly, which has the subtlety and style of a hungry barracuda. They don't just ease in to draw blood, like mosquitoes. They hit like torpedoes, apparently believing that they can carve out a hunk of flesh and blood and buzz off to horsefly heaven before you can react. I can't believe that this technique ever works, since the sudden shock of the attack invariably leads to instant death at the hands of the pained victim, but who am I to question strategies worked out through evolution? Maybe it does work on horses though, whose tails are probably less lethal than human hands. Poor horses.

I'm developing my insect-swatting skills with a wet t-shirt, sweating up the trail while trying to figure out where I am on the map. By late afternoon I've passed the last bridge, where the river cascades down the mountainside, when after a snack and water break I discover a dead tree branch perfectly suited to be my climbing staff, just in time.

Now I'm starting to pull uphill. I realize that the trail is no longer easy and I should have refilled the water bottles at what will be my last contact with the river for several miles. By early evening I'm dehydrated and just pushing to make a decent campsite before dark, when I finally pull over a steep grade to see the headwaters braiding down the mountainside, and an open meadow next to what is now a stream. Scanning the scene with an eye both for the sudden high mountain view and for a place to throw a tent, I find my first wilderness-quest site nestled up against the mountainside.

I watch the sun go down on the high mountain valley as I finish my first dinner of summer sausage, cheese, and nuts. Earlier I'd drifted dry flies down the stream on my new Winston rod and seen no sign of fish. Now I'm swatting mosquitoes and contemplating what exactly I have in mind by thinking I'm on some kind of "wilderness quest." Is it just a vague romantic overlay to a solo backpacking trip? Am I sincerely questing for revelations about my own nature and my relationships to the world? Am I secretly hoping for or fearing some supernatural visitation from spirits? Seeking some personal epiphany that will reshape my life?

So maybe a spontaneous solo backpacking trip is not a true wilderness quest at all, maybe it's just a fishing trip disguised as a half-assed vision quest, but whatever I'm doing I've decided to utilize what I know while observing my own limits. I've read a lot about different kinds of wilderness quests, both fictional and real, and I've learned some meditation techniques through years of studying Tai Chi Chuan, an internal Chinese martial art system based on Taoist philosophy. And just making the hike will push me to my limits physically and mentally, which seems to be a requirement for wilderness epiphanies. So for now I've decided that the main thing is just to be up here alone, to meditate as well as fish, to be open to whatever happens. I've also come to suspect that visions and revelations come in many forms, so I'm simply listening for messages, paying attention.

All of which is fine, but my first meditation never really deepens because as the sun sets, the mosquitoes start to swarm. My body aches and I crawl into my sleeping bag anticipating a serene night's sleep before the big push in the morning over the mountainside to Wounded Man Lake. I'm fourteen miles up in the wilderness on my own, and for the first time in my backpacking experience I think I hear noises from some large, shambling animal—like, for instance, a bear.

Maybe it's just the wind. Or maybe it is a bear snuffling around the nearby tree, trying to get at the sack suspended just out of its grasp on the bear rope, now glaring in frustration at my tent, catching a hint of fishy aroma from my nearby waders as the wind shifts . . . I even crawl out of my tent to check it out, look at the stars blazing in the night sky, then try again to sleep.

I'm up early the next morning, eager to get to the lakes. The hike up into alpine country is gorgeous but steep. I stop frequently for breath, and my pack feels like the weight of things I can't even fathom. By a little after noon my legs are shaky but I've arrived.

Wounded Man Lake sparkles in a high wooded plateau surrounded by mountain peaks. When I finally pitch camp and get to the lake with my fly rod I discover that the fish are surprisingly selective little rainbows, and that my back is so sore from hiking that I can't fish for long without a break. My day-hike to Lake Martee the next day fizzles when I decide I'm too unsure of my ability to follow the bushwhacking trail to risk getting lost, so I catch a few more rainbows at Wounded Man Lake and decide just to give up and head home the next morning.

That night I lie awake in the pitch dark of my tent battling despair and incipient signs of panic, trying to figure out why I'm here now that I've abandoned my spectacular fishing dreams. My legs and back begin to cramp and I'm feeling a little sick, wondering if I should have brought some salt pills like those we took when sweating heavily during high school football, trying to imagine what I would do if I really got too sick to make the seventeen miles back down the trail. For some reason the lake's name runs insistently through my mind. Who was the Wounded Man? I wonder. What wounded him? Did he come here to heal or to die?

Since I can't sleep anyway I'm up before dawn to break camp and climb up the ridge in the early morning chill. I'm shaky at the top but feeling good, knowing it's a steep downhill grade for the next four miles. I've never understood people who say that going downhill is as hard as going up, but now I realize that although climbing downhill is less work, it's also more treacherous. I'm easing down a rough section, relying on my staff for balance, when I hear a woman's voice with a cute, lisping accent call out behind me. "Passing."

It's another couple. He's from France and she's from Switzerland, and they glide by after our brief talk as though they're airborne, wearing enchanted boots that scarcely touch the earth. Light packs, I observe, marveling at their pace. Maybe they grew up doing this in the Alps, and their bodies are streamlined to move with the mountain winds.

As I continue my descent, thankful for the stout staff, the refrain begins in my mind. "Lighten your load. Lighten your load." I'm enjoying the sparkling view descending from alpine, trying to imagine what I could have left behind. Some of the clothes, surely. Some of the food. Maybe the fishing gear, as it turns out—but wasn't fishing the main point?

My foot catches on a protruding root and suddenly I'm face down in the trail, pinned under the weight of my pack, as helpless and stunned as an upended turtle. I've just fallen for the first time while carrying a backpack, something I thought could never happen to me. After figuring out how to wriggle out from under the pack, hoping no one comes along to see me in such an ignominious position, I scramble to my feet to take inventory. Scraped skin, but no real damage—nothing broken or sprained.

I look over the cliff edge next to me, shuddering as I try not to imagine what would have happened if I'd slid off the trail. I could have been the wounded man, I realize, dying broken and solitary on the cliff side below, pinned helplessly on the steep slope beneath the weight of my pack.

I move more carefully through the next few miles downhill, still hoping to make the nine miles back to Breakneck Park Meadow to pitch camp, but now the name itself seems a warning not to rush. And by the time I cross the bridge where I found my wilderness quest staff I listen again to the roar of the river, gaining confidence with every stride. I am going to make it, I'm thinking. This is now my fifth day on the trail and I can feel that my body is leaner and stronger, adjusted to the weight of the pack. I've learned that I can survive on summer sausage and cheese, but my food's looking a bit grimy by now, and I start to imagine the taste of a rare steak and cold beer at the end of the trail.

> If you ever go across the sea to Ireland,
> You'll know that with the breaking of your day . . .

I actually start to croon a few soulful bars of "Galway Bay" when I notice a subtle presence in my thoughts, and in my mind's eye I see my father's face. His expression reminds me of a few rare times when he seemed to lighten up with a kind of boyish enthusiasm. He doesn't speak in words, but I feel his emotions through his eyes. "This is really something, what you're doing," they seem to say, and I know he's here to provide encouragement and strength.

An old sadness wells up inside me and then washes away. I'd felt that there was a message for me in the way he died of cancer two summers earlier, that in some mysterious alchemy of suffering and forgiveness of himself and others he'd found a way to lighten the burden of a heavy story passed down through generations, especially from fathers to sons. And now his enthusiasm makes me grin. Maybe he's here to help me lighten the load of this western manhood story that I inherited through him. Memories flood back as I work carefully down the trail.

"Dad was a good father, but he wasn't what people today would call affectionate."

We're sitting at the kitchen table in the Idaho home a few summers before they diagnosed his cancer. I've been taping some of his reminiscences about the old ranching days. I've just finished a late snack of apple pie while he sips on a cup of coffee—a habit he and Mom shared with everyone of their generation, it seemed, sipping all day on what I considered weak Folgers coffee simmering in the percolator that was always on.

I'm surprised. He'd never really talked about Grandpa Slim in such a personal way before. He looks away as he struggles to find the right words, obviously uncomfortable, yet determined to say what he has to say.

"He was never mean to us kids, and we admired and respected him. He'd spank the hell out of you if you screwed up, but everybody's parents did back then. He was popular with the other men. He'd worked with a lot of them going back to his early cowboy days before he got married. He didn't talk much except when he was with them, but he could tell a good story.

"But he wasn't the kind of dad who would pick you up and hold you or set you on his knee. He was—well, I guess you could say he was distant. His parents died when he was eight, you know, and the people who raised him kind of treated him like free labor."

I'm remembering how Dad did play with us when we were kids, but some of his games were a kind of horseplay, cowboy pranks that could get carried away. He convinced my two-year-old brother Mike that he controlled the weather and time of day.

"Dad, don't make it dark. We want to play some more." Mike is breathless from running into the house from the backyard.

"Okay, Mike, but just for half an hour. Then I've got to start shutting down the lights so people can get some sleep. I'll hold off this rain until you kids are done." I look out the window to see the clouds forming on the horizon. I'm seven, old enough to figure out what he's doing. But he's so convincing I half believe him anyway unless I catch myself.

"Wow! Dad, how did you make the pie so fast?"

I was in awe. I'd checked in before dinner to see when Dad's stew would be ready. He'd just started chopping vegetables and meat. "I'm going to pick up your mom at the hospital," he'd announced. "I might just throw a cherry pie together before I leave."

Less than half an hour later, he has just come through the door with Mom, still in her starched white uniform. The stew steams in the pressure cooker, and the pie cools on the table.

"Oh, it doesn't take long for a man to make a pie," he ex-

plains. I notice a hint of exasperation in my mother's glance at him as she leaves the kitchen to change. He lowers his voice, speaking in confidence, man to man.

"Now women make a big production out of making a pie, patting the dough, making it just right. But if a guy just wants to make the pie and get the job done, it doesn't take long."

"I swear," I explain to the younger kids as he carves the pie after dinner, "Dad must have made that pie in about five minutes." They are as impressed as I am. Mom doesn't say a word. She just looks at Dad with a glint in her eye as we shower him with compliments.

That night I notice the frozen pie container in the garbage basket under the sink. Something I'd never seen before. And the pie didn't taste like the ones Mom makes, I reflect. It was sort of thin and tasteless. I push the frozen pie container down farther into the trash, hoping none of the younger kids will figure out that I've been fooled.

Dad looks at me sideways with a wry grin I'd rarely see, when he'd struggle to express something close to his heart.

"Dad never really gave compliments, but you could tell he was proud of you sometimes when you did good work. I suppose the closest he came to actually saying something to me was one time after I was grown up." His face softens as he tells the story.

"It was when your mom and I drove down to the ranch to visit after the war. You were just a baby, and he'd just met Mom and you for the first time. He and I were drinking coffee in the kitchen and he walked to a dresser and took a little knife out of the drawer.

"'Remember this?' he asked. 'You won that race at the county fair when you were seven, and they gave you this

knife as a prize. You ran a hell of a race that day.' I had no idea he'd kept it all those years."

I can't think of anything to say, an unusual experience for me.

"Well, hell, I'd better go check that hose in the potatoes."
He sets his cup down on the sink, pulls on his beat up old straw cowboy hat, and heads out the door. For the first time I realize how much he must have struggled to preserve his father's strengths, but to loosen up and actually have fun with his kids. He'd whale on me and Phil sometimes when we were young, but he lightened up on the younger kids.

"Thanks, Dad," I'm thinking. "Good to hear from you." I gaze down at the roaring current under the bridge, knowing that I'm now just two miles from the meadow where I'll pitch camp. I guess this is turning out all right after all.

I arrive at Breakneck Park Meadow by late afternoon, surprised to discover that I'm the only one there. I sprawl on my back in the grass by the river, soaking up the sun, the long trail and the emotions of the visitation from my father still throbbing through my body. After setting up camp I notice a swirl in the river, then another, and when I set up my Winston and drift a small caddis fly through the riffle, a brilliant jade and ruby rainbow slashes it, and then races up and down the stream until I settle it into my hand to release the hook. The trout are back, and I love the elegance and flexible strength of my new rod as I work up and down the bend. I release half a dozen more trout before I settle in for my last night's sleep on the trail, knowing that by this time tomorrow night I'll have left it all behind.

And then it's the next day, the last day, with five miles behind me, when I pull into a turnout where the trail hovers
over the Stillwater, and I meditate deep into the crystal clarity of the water on a still point for what seems forever but
isn't. I sit cross-legged beneath an ancient ponderosa with
huge gnarled roots that embraces everything in its timeless
presence. And later, when I'm a half mile farther down the
trail, I realize that I left my staff behind. I almost decide to
go back for it before I realize that it's where it should be,
that if I brought it out of the wilderness to my truck it would
be just another stick. Maybe another traveler will find the
magic staff after gazing forever into the Stillwater beneath
the giant pine.

I feel like I'm wearing seven-league boots coming down
the last mile to the trailhead, striding out like a horse heading for water and oats at the end of a long day. I give trail
and fishing news to other backpackers along the way, some
looking a bit apprehensive about what's ahead. The trailhead
seems a small city when I arrive, with several groups of backpackers and a major horse-outfitter operation all preparing
for the trail. After he asks where I've been an old cowboy
with a thick white handlebar mustache, who says he's traveled these trails since he was a boy, tells me stories while he
cinches up packs for the horses, about the huge Goldens at
Lightning Lake, and how some backpackers illegally fish
their spawning beds in the river.

I find my keys then throw my backpack into the camper
shell of my truck. Without the weight my body feels like it
floats, and for the first time in a week I'm moving down a
road on wheels instead of on my hiking boots, savoring each
mile of forest road as I estimate how long it would take to

walk it, as though I'm operating on trail time and road time simultaneously.

When I finally arrive at Absarokee I find an old style western restaurant with a huge mirror behind the bar, and I call Billings to let everyone know that I'm out and will be there for dinner. In extreme re-entry mode, a kind of schizophrenic trance suspended between worlds, I savor the first swallow of cold beer from a frosted mug. Everything around me seems wondrous and strange—the old cowboys ordering hamburgers and drinks, the country song from the jukebox, the bright colors and shapes reflected in the mirror.

I remember the stones etched in the bed of the Stillwater River, and as the beer flows through my body the translucent river water breaks up into bubbles that float to the top of my glass. It's beginning, I think, watching the light refract through the amber beer. It's already slipping away.

By the time I get to the truck stop at Laurel it's around a hundred degrees in the Yellowstone valley in the height of tourist season. I wait in lines to pump gas and pay my bill and gulp down cold juice that tastes impossibly delicious to quench a suddenly insatiable thirst as I fight through traffic on the sweltering freeway. And when I arrive in Billings we all go out to dinner—my brother Kirk and his family, and my mother, who's relieved to see I'm okay, and my brother Phil and his wife, Kathy, who have just flown in from their home in the Philippines.

It's great to be with family, joking, filling each other in about what's happening in our lives. I tell stories about the trip that are mostly true but seem to miss the point, trying to savor everything from the buffet at the Chinese restaurant and enjoying it all. But somewhere inside I'm trying to hold onto a vantage point from a still place inside all the sensations of sound and taste. And finally I call Liz, whom they had the good sense not to tell about my being alone on the trail, to let her in on the story too, and to plan my return home.

Now I'm awake in the middle of the night trying to capture something in words before it slips away, something I know I can't exactly describe though it was as real to me this morning as the staff in my hand. Something to do with living in time with the rising and setting sun, working hard all day on the trail, finding a spot, setting up a home, sleeping when the sun goes down and starting the day when it returns. Something about eating simply and drinking only water and feeling exhausted and sore but leaner and stronger each morning. Something I want to hold on to that cannot be held any more than the river can be held in the hand, but something that can be seen and known at least in glimpses, like those brilliant river stones seen through moving water.

And it's really all right that it's slipping away now, as I begin to drift toward sleep. Those places and stories are there inside me, where I can find the crystal clarity and otherworldly river stones when I need them. And now there's just the motion of the water, the river that flows through everything though it cannot be seen. It's all right to drift in this current that flows into morning, on this present moment like a floating piece of bark that carries us from our past into our future. That was the vision, I realize. Not just the river stones or my father's presence, but the whole thing, from the time I set off on my own until now. And I drift out of time itself toward those wondrous other worlds that we enter through sleep.

Will the Circle be Unbroken?

It's the morning of Christmas Eve 2001, and the funeral has just begun. Father Dave stands back from the makeshift altar in the funeral home as my brothers and sisters and I, set up with microphones and guitars to the side, lead everyone assembled there into the old hymn. As I begin singing my verse I feel the connection that the song creates between us all—the grandchildren, the in-laws, a few family friends who received notice in time to attend, Dad's youngest sister, Mabel, who introduced us to Father Dave, and the four members of Mom's family who drove down from Plentywood the night before. All joined in the mournful cadences of the verse.

> Undertaker please drive slow.
> For this body you are carrying,
> Lord, I hate to see her go.

Mom's body lies in the casket by the entrance to the funeral home, clothed in her favorite rose dress. Her hands, folded over her heart, clasp the rosary that had been blessed by the Pope. I feel her there in spirit, proud and peaceful, appreciative of the music and the ceremony, her presence gently touching everyone—reassuring, calming, savoring this union in her honor of most of the people she was close to who are still alive.

Mom had died so suddenly that we didn't have time to prepare. I had received the phone call from my sister-in-law just
four days earlier.

"David, this is Kathy. I hate to tell you this, but Thelma
was hit on 24th Street by a pickup truck just a couple of
hours ago. Kirk and Phil are both with her at St. Vincent's
Hospital."

"Good God, Kath. How bad is it?"

"Well, I don't want to worry you more than is necessary,
but it sounds like it could be pretty bad. You might think
about coming up a couple of days early for Christmas if
you can."

We'd all been planning to arrive in Billings a few days later
anyway for the holiday reunion, but there was enough ur-
gency in Kathy's voice to convince me to drive up the next
morning just to be with Mom and my brothers and their
families. My youngest sister, Helen, who as an RN was determined to be there immediately, left from Colorado Springs
even earlier than I did, and she and my nephew Philip were
already there when I arrived late that afternoon.

I assumed that we'd be able to talk to Mom, and then discuss her prognosis for recovery with Helen and my brothers
Phil and Kirk and some of the medical staff. I knew Mom
was pretty banged up and that she'd fractured her pelvis,
but I wasn't prepared to see her battered and blue and in a
coma, apparently unaware of who was or wasn't there, just
struggling to breathe. We arrived in the late afternoon and
watched her condition deteriorate over the course of the evening. I could tell that both Helen and my youngest brother,
Kirk, a respiratory therapist at the other Billings hospital
across the street, were worried.

In a family with more than its share of health professionals I'm probably the most squeamish when it comes to dealing with blood and mucus and pain, so for me that evening was a kind of nightmare which I had never imagined could come true. The respiratory therapist was trying to get a tube down Mom's nose to suction her lungs, and my job was to hold her left arm and shoulder so that she couldn't pull at the tube. Her body was reacting with all the strength she had left, which wasn't much by then. As I held her bruised shoulder and shattered arm firmly to the bed I averted my eyes from her face. I couldn't stand to watch. But there was a moment when I felt a spasmodic tremor through her body and looked up. Her eyes seemed to light up with startled recognition, as though she had just re-entered her body to look around at all of us in shock and wonder.

When we finished the ghastly procedure I looked again at her face as the respiratory therapist put his equipment away. She looked gray and drawn, still gasping for breath, and I thought, "My God, she looks like she's dying." But the hospital staff seemed to think she was doing fine, so I assumed my premonition was just due to my inexperience. Philip and I left at midnight to get some sleep, leaving Helen—who seemed distracted and distraught—to spend the night with her until the rest of us could get back in the morning.

"Let's look for her picture," Philip said, as we walked through the hallway to the hospital entrance, past the chronologically arranged photos of graduated nursing classes.

"Here it is." He'd located the St. Vincent's Hospital Nursing Class of 1941. A small group, and beaming in their midst, smiling shyly but glowing and beautiful, it seemed to me, was my mother. Thelma Wilson, Plentywood, Montana—proudly wearing her starched white uniform. That was when she and Dad were still courting, I realized. The graduating nurse and the ex-cowboy just beginning study at nearby Eastern College, before Pearl Harbor and World War II swept them away from Montana and everything they had known.

Philip and I walked into her apartment after midnight, surveying the materials laid out across the kitchen counter that she'd never had a chance to straighten out. There were the brochures about her new apartment in the independent living complex where she had planned to begin the new year. She'd fallen at the intersection at 24th Street earlier that fall, and had decided it was finally time to follow her children's nagging advice and move into a retirement community where she wouldn't have to negotiate walking through traffic on her own. She had finally accepted that it was time to move, and now that she'd selected a place she even showed signs of enthusiasm about it. We all imagined her playing bridge and talking about children and grandchildren and books with new friends. In a few more days we all would have begun to arrive, and she'd never again have had to cross 24th Street by herself.

Philip and I chatted as we looked through the materials then decided to get some rest. We had just settled in when the phone rang.

"I think you'd better come back up here," Helen choked out. "I'm afraid Mom's dying."

As we arrived the code-blue emergency convergence of nurses and doctors at her bed was just ending. Mom had died. In the midst of all the activity around her bed, her body was still. We all looked on, frozen in disbelief. I held Helen when she suddenly turned to me, shaking and sobbing.

We paid our respects to her battered body in the bright

light of the hospital, then gathered at my brother Phil's home until the early hours of the morning, confused, questioning whether we could have done more to insist on getting her to emergency care. We finally drifted back to our homes and motel rooms to sleep. We spent the next couple of days sorting through her belongings, telling stories, arranging for the funeral on short notice on Christmas Eve.

During the service Aunt Mabel and the Plentywood group led the responses to the Catholic Mass. I was surprised to realize that it was comforting and still familiar to me, though fundamentally altered by the change to English from the Latin I remembered as a kid, much of which I had memorized without ever really knowing the translations. *Ad Deum qui laetificat*, I remembered chanting, never at all certain what the words meant. And, striking my breast with each phrase of a passage whose translation I did know to register heartfelt repentance or sorrow, *Mea culpa, mea culpa, mea maxima culpa*. I am sorry, I am sorry, I am most grievously sorry.

Father Dave had assured us during our initial consultation that it was fine for non-practicing Catholics and non-Catholics to take Communion, so I took the sacrament for the first time since I was a teenager. Back then I'd believed that you could only receive the host if you'd just come from Confession in a state of absolute contrition. We concluded the Mass and sang our songs and spoke our tributes to Mom.

"My mother had many wonderful qualities," I remember saying to kick it off. "But the one I want to honor is just this. She was a great cook, like some of the other women here. She and Dad didn't have much money, raising six kids on his teacher's salary, but no matter how tough times were we always feasted on her farm cooking. There was always plenty of roast and potatoes and gravy and homemade cookies and pie, and the hospitality she and Dad extended to everyone who came to their home always centered on those wonderful meals." And my brothers and sisters and nieces and nephews spoke of her other qualities—the love and competence she brought to being a mother and nurse, her delight in discussing and sharing opinions about books, the special connection she would make by stroking your arm and hand while talking to you.

When we filed past her body I felt her presence embracing the room. She likes the way she looks in her rose dress with the rosary clasped against her breast, I thought, and she'll always be here in some way to give comfort and guidance. Then we gathered at the gravesite next to the one where the urn containing Dad's ashes is buried, and we said our last farewells as her coffin was lowered into the ground.

Riding the Hi-Line into the Past

Life has not been easy for anyone here and everywhere are the marks of skill, persistence, and heartbreak. These images [photographs] may suggest a place that's dying while that is not at all the case. It certainly requires many times 640 acres for a ranching family to survive and the population has thinned with time. Those remaining brave difficult seasons in a stunningly beautiful landscape. Towns still are inhabited by very resilient people who fully understand the limits and rewards of this challenging region.

> — BILL JAYNES of Bigfork, Montana,
> http://www.montanahi-line.net/

"Honyocker," Mom mutters while I light the barbecue, preparing to grill a salmon I caught off the Oregon coast on my way up from a seminar in Berkeley. "What an ugly name."

We're cooking dinner for our first real family reunion in the mid-1980s at my brother Mike's home in Coeur d'Alene, Idaho, all wearing these bright red t-shirts he had made up celebrating our "Hanyaker Reunion." Mike has created his own spelling since none of us have ever seen the word in print, and we assume it's simply a nonsense word from the old days that Dad used to tease us kids when we were young—a family inside joke that whimsically defines our identity.

Mom grimaces when she says the word, and I notice with surprise the intensity of distaste in her expression. I wonder what this is about, but she doesn't elaborate and never says anything further to dampen our enthusiasm for our reunion theme.

This all came back to me in the fall of 2003, after my sabbatical trip to eastern Montana to do more interviews and background research into the family heritage. After visiting with my brothers Phil and Kirk in Billings, I spent a couple of days with my cousin Ron Mogen, revisiting the Home Creek ranch and the graveyards in Forsyth and St. Labre Mission and Willow Crossing (out by a country road where no one could find it who didn't have clear directions). Having lived and worked in the Forsyth area for most of his life, Ron knows intimately these places and stories and the ways they intersect.

I headed north from Forsyth with a selection of old pictures, the original notebooks containing Grandmother Mogen's handwritten stories, and a box of my cowboy great-uncle Brian's letters and memorabilia that no one knew what to do with. I also had over a hundred pages of family genealogy, including short biographies of the vast network of descendants of the original Lynch family, assembled by Cathy Byron, one of my relatives who is especially dedicated to reconstructing family history.

Dad always loved to talk about the old ranching life. When he realized I had become fascinated by his stories he'd happily sit down in front of a tape recorder and reminisce about the old days. We even met one summer in Forsyth to team up with Uncle Bob and Great-Uncle Brian, travel to abandoned homesteads and schools and graveyards and videotape them, telling stories elicited by seeing the old places.

"That's what people do around here," Ron told me over coffee at his Forsyth home, in a tone tinged with weary resignation. "They talk about the old days. Who's related and how and all the stories that go with it."

But when I finally talked Mom into sitting down in front of the tape recorder to talk about her homesteading memories, she couldn't do it. She stammered out a few phrases about those early days being tough but good, and just couldn't go on.

"It's okay, Mom," I said. "Some other time." And in those years after Dad died, spontaneously, she finally did tell stories from her childhood. But always with this careful reserve, it seemed to me, as though there were secrets still to be guarded, hardships so severe that memories of them opened still-painful wounds and shame.

From Forsyth I drove north through the Missouri-breaks country to the far northeastern corner of the state, to Plentywood, which I had always thought of as Mom's hometown. But after spending a couple of days with Uncle Louie and Cousin Duane visiting the original family homesteads, I realized that though she'd gone to high school in Plentywood, Mom's childhood was spent in border country—some of it actually in Canada, and the rest of it in the community surrounding the small town of Raymond, just south of the Canadian border.

"I remember coming here after baseball games," I observe, suddenly flooded with memories. Cousin Duane has just driven through the two or three blocks that remain of Raymond, pointing out the large old building that had once been a thriving bar and restaurant. From the time I was fifteen I'd played shortstop and sometimes second base for the baseball team from Froid, just thirty-five miles south, back when all of these small farming towns still fielded baseball teams. Froid and Raymond were both part of the Big Muddy League, extending all the way east to Dagmar and south to Culbertson and west to Brockton on the Fort Peck Reservation—one of the last of the town-team leagues in the country, I later learned.

Unlike the high school teams in basketball and football, the town baseball teams represented the entire community, so at one point I played with a thirty-something local farmer on my right at third base and a recently arrived middle-aged farmhand on my left at second, who was reputed to have played some minor league ball before drinking destroyed his career.

With infield chatter we tried to instill fear in the hearts of batters facing our pitcher, a local farm kid whom we knew had spent some time in the minors, whose fastball and curve were the best in the league. We high school kids who played on the team traveled with the men to and from the games and afterward we hung out in bars, drinking sodas while men from both communities bought each other rounds of beer and ditches (whiskey and water on ice) and swapped stories.

Most of the local community came to the Sunday games, and most watched from their cars, since there were only a few rows of bleachers. They honked approval when someone on the home team got a hit or made a play in the field, while the kids ran around and played on the sidelines.

Duane drives down to the old baseball field nestled in next to a slough just southwest of town.

"It's been years since they've played a game here."

"Man, this was one of the prettiest baseball diamonds in the league," I recall, surprised at the vividness of my memories of the crowds and dust and thrills of the afternoon games, so distant now and yet so near.

Duane and Uncle Louie point out the area where Grandma Lena's old homestead had been, though nothing of the old buildings remains. We're driving to the old Heisler farm on the original homesteads of Grandma's brother Leo and "Grossmutter," as Mom always referred to her, in a tone that to me evoked images of a mysterious and intimidating matriarch. The Heisler farm looks tidy and cozy in the afternoon light, shaded by trees that also help break the wind. We visit with Leo's son Ed, who still lives there in retirement after his wife's death. What a quiet spot to have to yourself, I think, gazing out from the kitchen window at the trees and fields rustling in the wind. But pretty remote. It might be tough to get in and out during winter. I shiver at the thought.

"I don't know if you remember Thelma's boy, David," says Louie as he introduces us. Ed seems vaguely familiar to me.

"I'm not sure." He surveys me with a twinkle in his eye. "It would have been a long time ago, I guess."

"Ed used to play for the Raymond baseball team," observes Duane. As we sit down for coffee he recounts our visit to the old baseball field.

"What position?" I ask.

"Shortstop."

"Hey, maybe we played against each other. I played shortstop for Froid back in high school, from about 1961 through 1964, actually, the summer after my first year in college."

"Yeah, I think I was still playing then." His eyes flash at

the memory. He's still slender and energetic, and I seem to remember him as a younger man taking my spot at shortstop in the field while I ran to the team benches on the sideline.

That was over forty years ago, I realize, and all these farming communities I grew up in are dwindling. Most of the kids I went to school with have moved on, like all of us kids from my family. The old family homesteads have long since been consolidated into corporate farms or the larger and larger spreads of those who remain, worked by machinery that constantly increases in size and complexity. When Duane gave me a tour of his farmyard that morning I gazed up in wonder at the huge John Deere tractor, with its enclosed air-conditioned cab complete with a radio and sound system. The tool bar and disc it pulled covered at least twice the area of those I dragged through summer fallow back in the early '60s, singing to myself above the roar of the tractor to keep awake in the hot wind and sun.

I leave Raymond and Plentywood with a pile of documents about local and family history, my head and heart filled with new images and stories. I'd always imagined Mom's childhood on the farm to be somewhat serene and idyllic, a kind of pastoral gloss she usually applied when she did refer to it. Partially this was because when we'd lived in what I considered the same area in Froid in the late 1950s and early 1960s, life in these small towns had become relatively stable and comfortable. Looking back, I realize that that postwar era may have been the last great boom time for eastern Montana, when the original settlers' dreams of prosperous and expanding communities flourished.

But now I realize that however secure our world appeared in the post-war years, it was a radically different country for that first generation of settlers. And the area around Raymond where Mom grew up was border country, wild and wooly in ways I had previously associated primarily with Dad's ranching country, with its history of Indian wars, sheep and cattle wars (just south of there in Wyoming), and general frontier chaos.

After talking with relatives and browsing through materials on local history in the Plentywood library, however, I realize that when Mom grew up that country was just emerging from an era of cross-border horse-rustling only recently supplanted by the more profitable criminal industry of bootlegging. By then the region was flooded with newly arrived homesteaders who had eagerly staked claims throughout a territory that in the best of times was not well-suited to small farms, and in the worst could be ravaged for years by drought, ferocious winters, and the relentless wind.

But returning to this high-plains land has reminded me that it has its own seductive beauty. To those first settlers swarming in from across America and far places in Europe, this Montana Hi-Line country must have represented the last great chance to fulfill dreams about new beginnings, about owning land that could become home for generations to come, where children and descendants could flourish.

Before I leave that afternoon I talk for hours at the kitchen table with my aunt Ruth, wife of my mother's oldest brother, Uncle Joe, who passed away some years ago. At eighty-seven (Mom's age if she had survived), Ruth is still the strong, handsome farm woman I remember admiring as a kid, and she is both precise and reflective as I pursue answers to questions about people and stories that have emerged during my visit.

"Oh, why don't we eat some of these cookies," she says as she refills my coffee cup. "They're not the best I've made, but they're edible."

Two days earlier a group of us had sorted through family history for hours after breakfast—including Uncle Louie, and Ruth's daughter Valerie and her son Cory, who drove with me to his bank office to copy family history and genealogy materials brought by Alison LaGrange, another energetic relative who grew up near Mom on a neighboring farm, eagerly adding her information and memories to the post-breakfast stories.

"Ruth, here's the kind of story I never quite know what to make of," I observe after hours of animated discussion, realizing that it's getting later than I'd planned. I need to move down the road if I want to get to the Blackfeet Reservation the next day to meet with Uncle Gene and Mary Ellen and Conrad. "My sister Doris tells a story about Grandma Wilson going to a dance, sometime after she became a widow. She was dressed as a man and danced with some of the other women, who assumed she was a handsome stranger who'd just dropped in. Do you remember hearing about anything like that?"

Many of these social events seem to have been organized by the Non-Partisan League, a front group for the Communist Party. I'm intrigued by the combination of radical politics and gender-shifting cultural play in these simple old-time country dances.

"Oh, that could be," Ruth reflects. "Maybe she did dress as a man at one of our masquerade balls. Sometimes we had them at Halloween."

And perhaps that's all there is to it, I think, remembering

how suggestive and intriguing the story seemed when my sister Doris told it. But then she has a degree in Jungian psychology. Maybe sometimes a costume is just a costume.

I had just intended to stop by for a quick cup of coffee on my way out of town, but it's late afternoon by the time I leave Plentywood. As I head south through the small towns I'd passed through so many times back in high school—Reserve, Antelope, Medicine Lake, Homestead—my mind buzzes with memories and new stories. Aunt Ruth had talked about my grandfather Jim Wilson's desperate alcoholism (I never think of him—the most mysterious of my grandparents—as "grandpa"); about the hard times after his death when the oldest boys, her husband Joe and the second son Irvin ("Dutch"), still teenagers, ran the farm along with Grandma; about the conflict when a suitor proposed to her, when Joe and Dutch threatened to leave if she married, and essentially ran him off because they didn't think he'd take care of the kids. I'm trying to imagine the impact of all this intimate family conflict on a young girl.

On impulse I turn into Froid to see who's in the Mint Bar on Friday afternoon. I spend an hour reminiscing with the small group there in what seems a kind of elegy for times past. Wearing fatigues that he might have acquired during his tour in Vietnam, Will Warren, who'd been in my sister Doris's class and now seems a kind of unofficial town historian, describes the past and current condition of the kids I'd gone to school with. Pretty much all gone. More of them live in Billings now, it seems, than around Froid. When a familiar looking man with one arm steps through the door I recognize Timmy O'Leary, who owned the bar and the adjoining café back when they were the centers of the town's energetic social life.

"David Mogen," he says when Will introduces me. "Oh yes, Harold Mogen's oldest boy." Dad used to chat with him over coffee at his café before school opened in the morning. "Let me see, your sister Doris was one year ahead of my son Micky's class, I think."

"You're right. Hey, didn't Micky take over as quarterback that next year after I left for college?"

"Yeah, he did." His face lights up with memory. "Your Dad worked as a bartender for me here, that summer before he quit. I told him, 'Harold, as the school superintendent you can't tend bar in a small town like this,' but he just said 'Why the hell not?' By God, he wouldn't let those religious nuts tell him what to do."

Yes, but then he quit that next spring without even having applied for a position anywhere else, during my second year at Columbia, I think as I head south to Culbertson. And I've never really understood why he left the best job he'd had because of some criticism from fundamentalists, when he still had the support of most of the community. Some old cowboy reflex called "take this job and shove it while I ride off into the sunset," as far as I can figure, that probably works better for a lone rider than a teacher with a wife and six kids.

Maybe I should go back and talk to Timmy O'Leary about it sometime, I think, realizing how mystified I still am by Dad's abrupt decision. He'd never talked about it. He'd built a great small town school system there (which had gotten some recognition around the state), and he'd been elected vice president of the Montana Education Association, but after he quit things were never the same.

Turning west on Highway 2 out of Culbertson I begin the ride back over the Montana Hi-line, retracing in reverse the route my family traveled while I was growing up. I seem to be riding back into my past as I enter the Fort Peck Reservation east of Poplar, followed by Brockton and Wolf Point. Finally I arrive in Frazer, where I pull off the highway to find that the old brick school has been vacated for a new one, and the two bars and small grocery and drug store that made up what had been Main Street have been abandoned. The old log houses in the Indian section of town have been replaced by BIA-constructed ranch houses, so everything looks more modern than I remember. I wonder if the town is still divided into distinct white and Indian sections.

And then I drive out to Frazer Lake. The smell of the artesian springs along the old road leading to it is still there, but the lake itself, which I had once imagined surviving from the great inland sea of ancient millennia, has vanished. Surveying the lake bed filled with huge weeds gone to seed, I realize that it had always been a manmade structure, created by a dam. I remember the long summer days and weekends tramping through the brush, catching bullheads, and swatting with sticks at schooling carp.

Then I head west through Nashua, curving south to the Fort Peck Dam along a road a neighbor followed when he took me along with his family to fish for walleyes. After driving west to Glasgow, the "big city" in the region when we lived in Frazer, I pull into town as the evening light fades, find an attractive cheap motel room (one of the benefits of Montana's depressed economy) and savor memories of my visit along with prime rib at a local steak house.

The wind screeches the next morning as I blast across the Hi-Line, hoping the weather will change by the time I arrive at the Blackfeet lakes and Glacier Park mountains to the west. I pull into the Buffalo Hot Springs west of Saco, soaking in the hot pools that I remember from a spring school trip that Dad organized while we lived at Whitewater. As an eight-year-old I'd bounce out on my tiptoes to where the water was over my head, then dogpaddle back to the rest of the kids, feeling the warm mineral water melt the winter lingering in my bones.

As I float in the hot mineral water I drift back into my most recent memories of Whitewater. The summer after we were married I'd taken Liz on a tour of my old hometowns along the Hi-Line. Everything was still reasonably consistent with my memories—except for Whitewater, which I remember as suspended in the frontier past in a time warp. But by 1989 things had obviously changed.

The road from Malta was paved much farther north than I remembered. To my astonishment, a large road sign welcomed you to town, commemorating a recent State Championship in basketball. The old country store where we hung out for hours at a time as kids was replaced by an attractive new café with a bar. Out front kids in fashionable biking outfits secured their spiffy looking bikes to a bike rack.

"It's like a fancy bistro or something," I marveled to Liz.

"Well, I wouldn't go that far," she observed. "But it's not exactly the way I pictured it after your descriptions."

I introduced myself and Liz to the older fellow standing next to us at the bar.

"Harold's boy. David. Well, of course. I'm Duane Colter. You probably don't remember me, but I was on your dad's school board. He really turned our school around." This was Dad's first real success story before his years in Froid, I realized. He recruited some great young teachers. When we arrived in town I had shown Liz the school that Dad passed bonds to build, and provided a vivid account of the ancient structures, connected by a tunnel filled with salamanders, that it had replaced.

Duane and I compared memories, recounting with special enthusiasm the way Dad's new coach Jimmy Corr transformed the basketball team and got them into the semifinals at the tournament.

"What happened to Whitewater Creek?" I asked as we prepared to leave. "It looks dry. When we were kids we'd prowl along the banks for miles, flailing away at ducks and geese with rocks. Nobody ever hit anything, but we thought we were great hunters."

"It's been dry for years now," he sighed. "Too much pressure from irrigation, I suppose."

"Amazing," I observed to Liz on the way back to Malta. "Progress has come to Whitewater. The time warp is gone. I actually kind of liked it, I guess. But those days are over."

Still toasty from the hot springs I do something I rarely do, especially when I'm pushing to get somewhere beautiful for evening fly-fishing. Perhaps the mineral water has slowed me down, leaving me floating in memories. I pull over about ten miles east of Havre to read one of the large roadside signs that explain local landmarks and history. And there, on this weather-beaten old sign that I suspect stood there back when we traveled this road when I was a kid, I discover a clue to something I've been trying to comprehend about my eastern Montana heritage:

HURRY, HONYOCKERS, HURRY!

Emblazoned capital letters trumpet the word that echoed like affectionate nonsense through our childhood. But these honyockers were obviously in a great rush to get somewhere, and as I read the text that describes their quest I realize why my mother had reacted with such distaste to the word. She'd probably never read the sign, but she knew the story it told. The opening passage comes from a mid-century book about Montana history, Joseph Kinsley Howard's *Montana: High, Wide, and Handsome*, whose title implicitly casts the land itself in the role of the hero. Opposing the high handsome cowboy identified with the land is the ambivalent story of the "honyocker," etched in the splintered, windblown highway sign:

> Honyocker, scissorbill, nester. He was the Joad of a quarter of a century ago, swarming into hostile land; duped when he started, robbed when he arrived, hopeful, courageous, ambitious: he sought independence or adventure, comfort and security. Or perhaps he sought wealth . . .

These "swarming" honyockers—like clouds of locusts descending on the land. Perhaps valiant in their struggles but decidedly victims, duped dreamers at best, despoilers. A more measured contemporary history, *Montana: A History of Two Centuries*, wryly observes that Howard depicts "Montana's history from the cattleman's perspective and tended . . . to view the dirt farmers as rubes and hayseeds who despoiled the good earth." The authors even provide another definition for the term: "In its earlier usages 'honyocker' was a slur that was a corruption of a German expression meaning 'chicken chaser.'"

Next, the sign's text sketches in the outlines of the hon-yocker story:

> Promoted by railroad, by government, and by the American dream trainloads of newcomers rolled in and filed homestead entries. They fenced the range and plowed under the native grasses. With optimism born of inexperience and promoters' propaganda they looked forward to bumper crops on semi-arid bench land, but the benches never were meant for a Garden of Eden. There were a few years of hope, than drought with its endless cycle of borrowing and crop failure. Between 1921 and 1925, one out of every two Montana farmers lost his place to mortgage foreclosure.

"Honyockers." Homesteaders seen through threatened and contemptuous ranchers' eyes. Chicken-chasers foraging in an Eden periodically turned to dust. Losers and survivors, emblems of pursuing an American Dream as often illusion as reward. These were my mother's people, whose story seems a last great expression of the quest for home in a new frontier that has defined so much of American heritage, yet a story that somehow has evoked this shadow legacy of failure and shame.

For so many, the dream was just beyond their grasp. The story they lived promised success for pluck and hard work, which made the cost of failure not merely material but personal. That was the dark side of the American Dream: if success is available to all, only losers fail, and they have only themselves to blame. Perhaps my mother's reticence about speaking of her past measured the painful intensity of this frontier struggle for survival and respect. Dreams can inspire, but how do you heal the wounds left from broken dreams?

The honyocker quest for a new home brought my grand-mother Lena's family to Montana when she was seventeen. They actually arrived a year early, in 1909, after earlier travels had taken what remained of her family from their original home in Minnesota to Texas and then to Saskatchewan. Like the fragments of story I received through my mother, local history narratives often provide suggestive details without context, snippets of information that tantalize the imagination. I discovered an especially intriguing version of the honyocker origin story of my mother's family in a local history book, *Sheridan's Daybreak* (about Sheridan County, encompassing Plentywood and the numerous smaller towns in the northeast corner of the state). The account was written by her uncle Leo Heisler's wife, Gertie—known for her Irish fire and wit. She describes these early homesteading journeys with detail that is sparse, evocative, and sometimes even a bit bizarre:

> In June of 1909 she [Grossmutter Heisler] with her son Leo, and two granddaughters . . . packed all their belongings in a covered wagon and set out for Montana to homestead. This wagon was equipped with a cook stove, so they did their cooking along the way. . . . They had to stop to let the three horses and three cows graze on the grass. Water presented a problem. When they came to a slough of water this was their campsite. They camped near Estevan, Saskatchewan for several days waiting to see a circus that was showing there.

I envision a German-speaking matriarch with the youngest son of her twelve children and two granddaughters and three horses and three cows wandering across this vast expanse of windy and sparsely watered land, enjoying the luxury of their portable stove and stopping to frolic for a few days at a circus. That first winter they lived in a "sod shanty" that they apparently just stumbled upon, the narrative continues, but after discovering the next spring that their shanty home was on "Indian land" they headed in a "northeasterly direction" until one day Grossmutter Heisler, "spying a large slough of water," proclaimed, "'this is it' and she wouldn't go any further."

And so the original honyocker homestead was discovered, just south of the Canadian border. Here Grossmutter "started a grove of trees from seeds her dad gave her in Minnesota," and here she "spun her own wool into yarn" while her son Leo filed for an adjoining homestead, proceeded to break up sod with the team of horses, and began raising "cattle, horses, sheep, pigs, and chickens."

They suffered a tragic loss one Sunday, probably while traveling back and forth from a "Raymond grain elevator" where Catholic Mass was conducted and where Leo was "an adult when he was confirmed" because "visits of the Bishop were few." They returned to discover that "someone stole a team of horses and also took Rodney Salisbury's dress shoes from Mrs. Allen's shanty near by." When a pair of stolen shoes figures so prominently in such a sparsely detailed origin story, you realize that you are returning to a world where great value could be assigned to what now seem ordinary things.

Anyone who has survived winters up in this high plains country, even with insulation and central heating and cleared roads, knows the depth of hardship implied in stories such as these, yet the spirit that informs them often seems less grim than adventurous, and sometimes even joyous or droll. Will there ever again be such a harrowing but wondrous migration as this last flood of working class pioneers wandering the plains in search of the destined slough over the next rise of hills, the particular configuration of water and protection from the wind, that announces itself as the precise location of home in a vast new world?

But not all these stories resolve with such a definitive sense of even erratically fulfilled dreams. While Grossmutter and Great-Uncle Leo and their extended family made their homesteads home, his younger sister, my grandmother Lena, stayed in Canada. There she worked as a cook in a restaurant until 1912, when she married Jim Wilson and moved to Montana to homestead next to Grossmutter and Leo.

Both of my grandfathers remain mysterious figures to me, but Jim Wilson most of all. Dad's father, Slim Mogen (actually "Severt" originally), seems to have emerged on the Montana range like an orphaned Norwegian Huck Finn who found his true home at last on the cowboy frontier. All I know of his earlier life is that after his parents died of diphtheria on their homestead in Minnesota he and his brothers and sisters were distributed to anyone who would take them. In young Severt's case this was a family that essentially used him as a slave—Dad's word, at least, to describe his situation. One day when the farmer was gone on an overnight trip to town to get supplies Severt packed everything he owned into a sack that he threw over his back, announced to the farmer's wife that he was leaving, and headed west. He spent a winter in mountain country working with an old sheepherder before getting his first cowboy job working on the Bug Ranch in southeastern Montana.

All of which is probably too perfectly legendary to be entirely true, but at least I knew Grandpa Slim somewhat while I was growing up, and since some of his brothers and sisters sought each other out later in life, there was some sense of family connection. Dad always spoke with particular affection of his uncle Ole, who worked at ranches in the area while Dad was a boy, and always brought candy for the kids when he rode in for a visit. Reputedly when he first arrived in Montana, Ole searched out Grandpa at work on the range, rode up, and asked, "How are you doing, Severt?" and looked him in the eye until his younger brother, astonished, recognized him.

But of Jim Wilson I know practically nothing, except that he apparently was a charismatic alcoholic possessed of considerable wit and charm when he wasn't pitifully deranged by drunkenness. Aunt Ruth recalled hearing stories about him swatting at spiders crawling on his skin down by the railroad tracks next to the bar.

But the stories I have of him through my mother have a legendary quality of a different kind. Mom's sketchy accounts of her father seemed carefully guarded, perhaps wistfully romanticized, so that he appeared as a kind of displaced prince, a poignantly tragic figure. From an Irish family in Tennessee, he had come west because as the second son he couldn't inherit the family land, which Mom speculated might have been of considerable value because of some finely bred horses he had brought with him.

In 1919, while Mom was still a baby, they moved from the Montana homestead to Clear Lake, just across the border in Saskatchewan, which at that time was a local resort area.

From Cousin Duane's farm, just a mile from the custom house at the border, we drive about six miles to see what still remains. Duane and Uncle Louie are surprised to discover that they no longer maintain the playground and picnic areas, so that swings and slides now go to rust while the lawns return to native grass.

Back when my mother's family moved there, Clear Lake boasted a thriving night club with a dance hall and even horse racing, an environment in which I imagine Jim Wilson thrived until he died of pneumonia contracted from exposure in a blizzard during one of his binges. After his death in 1924, when Mom was seven, her mother brought them back to Montana to take up another homestead next to Grossmutter and Leo.

With some fondness Mom remembered her father getting her up from sleep to sing "Ka-ka-ka-Katy" for him and his friends while they were partying. She seemed to have forgiven him, as I suspect children in such situations yearn to do, and I always sensed a painfully unarticulated love and regret when she spoke of him. And once, after Dad was gone, reminiscence about her father revealed a connection between him and Dad that I had never imagined. "Well, he was a good man despite it all," she said. "And I guess I did find my own witty Irishman after all."

Mom may have sought to escape from her past in many ways, but she embraced it, too, and it seems to me now more than ever that the deepest contradictions she sought to resolve are embodied in the word "honyocker." It began as a label of contempt, but by the time we heard it as kids there was much to embrace in it as well. It evokes an ambivalent story, like the responses it evoked at our family "Hanyaker Reunion." Mom felt the shame and pain the word could inflict, but we kids had grown up thinking that being honyockers was kind of cool, and Mike's instinct to celebrate our honyocker identity had truth as well. The word could be an insult, but I suspect it often was used to establish a humorous common identity between people sharing a common fate. In eastern Montana during the Depression both the farming and the ranching economies collapsed, and small ranchers on their homesteads shared the same miseries as the honyocker farmers.

"Come on, you honyockers," Dad would yell, and we'd feel special. "Honyockers" sounded kind of wild and crazy but they were fun. They were down to earth and tough. They had a lot of energy and spunk.

Maybe Montana needs another road sign to tell the story from the honyocker point of view: HUNKER IN, HONYOCKER, AND HEAL! would be emblazoned across the top. And the text would speak of the resilience and good humor that sustain dreamers when dreams fail; of the satisfactions of winning small or just surviving as well as of winning big; of women who directed single household wagon trains and worked the family farm when husbands failed; of working class schools, and farmer's unions, and radical politics; of pride that endures being down and out to work for another day; of forgiveness that heals all wounds.

My trip across the Hi-Line ends in Blackfeet country, where the plains run into the Rockies. I take Uncle Gene and Mary Ellen and Conrad out to dinner in East Glacier at the Mexican restaurant, Mary Ellen's favorite. I also give them envelopes containing announcements from Mom's funeral service and copies of the taped interview I'd done with Uncle Gene two years earlier when I was last there, along with copies of the stories I had written about Dad's death and the Iniskim medicine gift that they gave to me. Uncle Gene seems in good spirits, though his hip bothers him more than it used to, and

Conrad is still recuperating from heart surgery. Mary Ellen scans the stories while we eat our burritos, seeming pleased with what she sees.

"Hey, why don't you come over to our place for dinner tomorrow night," she says. "You'll be surprised."

When I arrive at the end of the driveway by Cut Bank Creek, I decide I've pulled in at the wrong home, since the house doesn't look right. But after checking out several houses down the road I return, realizing that this has to be it. The door faces a different direction, and the house looks bigger. When I look through the window I see Mary Ellen working at the stove, and she gestures for me to come in.

"Wow." I walk in, surveying the shiny new wood floors and the newly redesigned kitchen. "There's so much more room, and it's so much lighter."

"Yeah," says Mary Ellen. "After all those years we decided to fix the place up. It was always so dark in here. And we did it just in time, since Conrad ended up spending so much time here after his operation. We even got him a new TV to watch while he gets better."

I chat with Conrad, alternately surveying the view through the new windows and on the snazzy new big-screen TV. I can tell he is still weak from the effects of the surgery, but he's working again and obviously enjoying getting back to normal.

"Good Lord, Conrad." I just noticed the soccer score flash on the big screen. "What are you watching?"

"We've gotten hooked on watching this British soccer team." He chuckles at my reaction. "Hey, it's not football, but it's pretty interesting once you get to know the teams."

"The score is zero to zero at the end of the third period.

It's soccer. It's British. Man, Conrad, you've had too much time on your hands."

"Manchester will get them in overtime," Mary Ellen says, as time expires. "That'll only take a couple of hours."

I remember that I'd teased her years ago, back when I'd first started visiting with them, about her fascination with the tragedy of Princess Diana and the ongoing drama of the British royals. "Mary Ellen, you're keepers of a Thunder Pipe bundle," I said. "Why do you care about all this Old World Brit stuff? You're wrecking all of my images about traditional tribal life."

"Well, we live right next to Canada," she replied half-seriously, as though she'd never really thought about it before. "So we hear about it all the time. We get all this British news from CBC. And, hey, most Blackfeet actually live in Canada."

All of which leaves me thinking, as I fish the Blackfeet lakes the next day before heading south the following morning, about time and space and history, and how even these seemingly objective things are shaped by our cultural perspectives and our stories. Here at the western end of the Hi-Line in Blackfeet country there's still an older geography co-existing with the places we know as Canada and America and Montana. The Montana Blackfeet are the southern tribe of the Blackfeet Nation, most of which is in what is now Canada, but that history goes back far before Canada and Montana ever existed, and may well continue after they're gone.

So most of these family stories I'm searching out may begin and end in Montana, but some, like the stories of my Blackfeet relatives, like the Iniskim story I received from them, may move in cycles in which the very concept of the frontier is only part of a larger circle of stories defining this place as home. And I make another cast in Ghost Lake, which is low and muddy because of several years of drought, hoping that by the time I return next year or in years after the lakes will be fishing again like they did those summers when I first discovered them. "Just bring them some good snow this winter," I ask of the clouds over the Glacier Park peaks, "so these Blackfeet fish can get plentiful and strong again."

Epilogue

Healing Dreams

"Everybody is against us," Paw said. "Everybody lied to us. It was better in Missouri."

Paw was right in one of his statements, wrong in the other. At least, the railroad lied. Their lying brochure was still somewhere in the house. It spoke of a new, rich land with ample water. One hundred and sixty acres for the man who had foresight to make the move. And so they came. Families from Wisconsin and Minnesota, from Iowa and Missouri. They were met with hostility from the cow- and sheepman, for each new plow meant that so much grass was forever lost. They were cheated when they bought materials and supplies. They were abused and derided, the Montanans called them Honyockers, lumping all races and origins in the one contemptuous term. The Slavic people, from Minnesota, were the first arrivals and were called Hunyaks. Ashel supposed Honyocker derived from that. Paw was right about people being against them, about people lying to them. But he was wrong about it being better in Missouri. . . .

He said flatly, "Maybe it wasn't any worse, but it wasn't any better."

—GILES A. LUTZ, *The Honyocker*,
winner of the Silver Spur Award, 1962

Thelma Wilson. The quiet one, according to surviving relatives and friends from Plentywood and Raymond who remember her as a girl. The reader. Her younger sister Roma was the talker, the playful one. But Thelma, she was so nearsighted before she got her glasses that she could hardly see anything. Except the books, the magazines, whatever in print she could get her hands on.

It's February 2004 and I'm contemplating this story about our Montana heritage that I began reconstructing long before my parents moved back to Billings for Dad's final months. To me there's something beautiful about the fact that they returned to the Yellowstone River country where they first met, and are now buried there together. My own quest to understand our western past really began with hearing stories about my father's ranching country. But perhaps I've been searching all along to recover a more elusive story from the Montana homes I left behind. Now I realize that for me the story begins with seeking to understand my father's south-eastern Montana cowboy heritage, but it ends with returning to the Hi-Line farming country where I grew up, reconstructing my grossmutter's, grandmother's, and mother's quest to build a home.

Contemplating Mom's life and death brings me back to the honyocker story, the hidden story. My father's ranching story, transcribed through countless novels and memoirs and films and television series, has become a central myth. But my mother's story, going back to that first generation that flooded into northeastern Montana in the country's last great Homestead Boom in the second decade of the twenti-eth-century—that story I'm still piecing together from fragments and hints.

At our first family reunion after Mom's death—which brings home to me the strange fact that I am now the elder member of the family—I ask my sisters if they're willing to discuss Mom's life and their memories of her on tape. I've realized that much of what I know about her early life has come through my sisters, and looking back it seems to me that there was always an unacknowledged women's circle within the family, which would be most evident when they would sometimes converse at length in Mom's bedroom while we men would read or watch sports or discuss politics. I'm curious to hear Mom's story through their voices.

My brother Mike has rented a multi-bedroom beach house on the Oregon coast—the first time we've ever pooled our resources to do something so lavish—and when my sisters begin speaking into the microphone, with the surf and the sounds of guitars and family singing in the background, I reflect on how far we are from the prairie homes where Mom grew up. As Doris and Helen pass the microphone between them their voices weave together stories that I've heard and others that I haven't in detail, with perceptions that I'd never imagined, so that for the first time I feel a coherent connection between the woman we knew as Mom and her homesteading past.

Sometime in those early years, Doris begins, the family was afflicted by scarlet fever, and Mom was nearly given up for dead. When the doctor arrived at the homestead, Grandma Lena and the older boys were so weak that he was worried none of them would make it. He told Grandma that she'd best let Mom pass away to concentrate on saving the others, since he didn't think she would survive in any case. Grandma didn't give up and Mom survived, but the disease affected her eyesight so severely that years later, when she was given an eye exam in which they asked her to read letters on a blackboard, she asked where the blackboard was. When she finally got glasses she walked around in wonder, realizing that she hadn't really been seeing the world that everyone else saw.

Though Mom always remembered her father with devotion, his alcoholic binges kept them in poverty and chaos when she was a young girl. Periodically Grandma Lena took the kids and left him, but she always returned. And after he died in 1924, when Mom was seven, her mother ran the farm with the help of the older boys, so in an area where times were tough for everyone they grew up as the children of a single mother who never remarried.

Grandma Lena worked in the fields with the boys, but at some point she also took a job cooking and cleaning at a neighboring farm so that they could have some cash income. So from the time she was a young girl, Mom took care of the younger kids at home and did heavy chores. She remembered carrying her younger brother Louie out to her mother in the fields to be nursed, during one period, and she developed a close relationship with the family cow that she milked and cared for.

"My God," Doris exclaims, bursting into laughter as she remembers her surprise at the vividness and humor with which Mom told some of these stories. "When I was a girl I never imagined my mother having such a meaningful relationship with a *cow*. She called it by name, but I can't remember what it was."

Doris took Mom back to Plentywood the summer before she died, and she was struck by the intensity of Mom's responses to some of the places they visited. As they approached the old Heisler farm Mom asked her to stop by a particular hill.

"'Oh my Lord,'" she said—Doris's tone transmits the shock in Mom's voice as the memory comes back to her. "'This is where we killed the rabbits.'"

Mom described to Doris how the entire community had joined into a kind of hunting ceremony to combat a rabbit infestation. The men and boys formed a huge circle, miles in diameter, carrying sticks and bells and anything that would make noise, then converged to the center, where the girls and women waited with clubs and farming implements to kill the rabbits as they fled. I'd read references in local history to such rituals, which always seemed to me outlandishly strange, but until Doris's account I'd never imagined what the impact would be on a young girl at the center of the slaughter.

As they round off discussion of Mom's childhood Helen asks if we've ever noticed the print of the painting, "Song of the Lark," that decorates a wall of their home. "It reminds me of Mom as a young girl," she says. "I can imagine her in the prairie like that, with the wind in her hair, listening so intently to the sound of a bird."

Now I can, too, but I realize what a revelation it is for me to fully imagine Mom back in that time. While I grew up she seemed so totally a 1950s housewife, always pregnant and dealing with sick kids and laundry and ironing and cooking and cleaning. And I'd never had any idea what it meant to her to be a nurse.

She and her younger sister Roma left the farm to attend high school in Plentywood, an opportunity which was not taken for granted by farming kids at the time. But they were both excellent students. Mom's gifts in reading and writing had been recognized earlier when she'd been asked to serve as secretary at some of the radical political meetings in the area. And she seems to have known early that she wanted to be a nurse. After graduation she spent a year working and saving money to buy a uniform and decent clothes for school, then applied to the nurse's training program at St. Vincent's Hospital in Billings.

Doris thinks Mom and Roma had a kind of pact to work together to leave northeastern Montana behind, at least partially to escape the stigma of growing up without a father in a time and place when single mothers, even widows who chose not to remarry, stirred gossip and suspicion. And I wonder if she didn't carry throughout her life that resolute purpose to escape her past and establish a stable home, so that her deepest instinct as a mother was to provide the stability and security she'd rarely known as a child.

I was finishing graduate school when Dad retired and they moved to Idaho, where Mom returned to nursing full-time, and during that time I began to realize how important her profession was to her. But from my sisters I learned how deeply she had regretted having to abandon her career to live in the small towns where Dad taught, and how important it was to her to move to Ennis in the years after I left, because there she could work in a hospital again.

In Rupert Helen worked with her as an LPN in the local hospital, and she speaks with wonder of the transformation she observed when Mom put on her uniform and walked on the floor. She was organized and precise and very much in charge, but she'd also developed a deep intuitive sense of her patients' experience. Both Doris and Helen have experienced this directly, since they both were under her care with severely broken legs at different times while she worked in the hospital at Ennis.

"She was the only one I wanted to move me," says Helen, who was eight years old and in traction at the time, "because the pain was so unbearable. But she would know exactly how to touch me, or she'd know how to organize the others to help her." And they describe Mom's unusually personal approach to nursing, how she would focus on each of her patients to imagine their experience, and then follow her intuition about how to minimize their pain and soothe them.

As her son growing up I had no idea that my mother was a kind of artist at her chosen profession, but when Helen spoke at her funeral about the way she would stroke your arm when she spoke to you I'd realized she had a healing touch both as a nurse and as a mother. I remember the way she'd intuitively known to stroke the buffalo rock Iniskim when I presented it to her, like the medicine woman in the story.

And now I realize that my mother was part of a vast network of healing women present in the background of many of these frontier stories, women who sustained families and communities by cooking on a wagon stove while searching for a home as they wandered through a forbidding new land, who wove cloth from wool and created their own patterns from which to sew clothes, who worked behind horse-drawn plows when necessary, and served as midwives for each other in birth and cared for the sick and dying with boiling water and linens and whatever home potions and remedies they possessed. And I realized that many of those small-town 1950s housewives carried with them into their modern homes wisdom and knowledge passed down through generations of pioneer women who helped their families survive by making do with whatever was at hand, to create homes out of places, and to heal the wounded.

All of these wounds from broken dreams, this healing that sometimes only comes with death and new life. I remember another conversation the night before I left Plentywood, when my uncle Louie and aunt Margaret, who grew up across the border in southern Saskatchewan, took me to visit Mary Stenson, another relative who grew up near the old homestead. We ate her homemade cake and sipped coffee as I talked to her and Louie about what they remembered of the old homesteading life. They wove through stories about rough winters and country school and bizarre characters, but at the end of it Mary leaned back in her chair and sighed.

"You know, we always make it sound like such hard times, but to me that's really not the way it was. We were all in the same boat. We pretty much always had enough to eat and warm clothes and lots of kids to play with, and nobody knew that it was supposed be any different. I guess we didn't have much, but in a lot of ways those were good times to grow up."

And now I listen to my sisters' voices round off my mother's story as the tape winds down, and I notice how they end with laughter. I wonder if that is in some ways the most healing touch of all.

"Oh my Lord," Helen says, "I just remember laughing so hard with Mom sometimes, especially when Roma came to live with us after she finally left Uncle Phil, or when I was younger sometimes talking with her and Grandma Lena. The goofiest things would get us going, and Mom, you know how she'd cover her mouth when she laughed because when she was younger she had a space between her teeth she didn't want people to see? She'd laugh so hard, shielding her mouth with her hand, that tears would come to her eyes."

And I remember a night here in Colorado at a New Year's Eve party in our home, just a few years before Dad was diagnosed with cancer. Many of our friends were here, and Liz's colleagues from work arrived unexpectedly just before midnight with more bottles of champagne. I looked across the crowded room after we made the New Year's toasts to see Helen and Mom leaning in to talk to each other at the table in the corner of the kitchen. Mom's hand covered her mouth and they were so convulsed with laughter that they look like they might fall off their stools. Full-body laughter. And then I remember a curious experience I had years earlier while lecturing in Poland.

The USIA staff at the embassy in Warsaw had put me on a train to Poznan to deliver my last lecture, so after several days of teaching and speaking at other universities across the country, always traveling with an escort, I was traveling alone for the first time in a country where I didn't know the language. I had located a corner where I could sit by myself in a passenger car with seats facing each other, designed for comfortable conversation. I observed the scenery through the window, reflecting on how much it reminded me of the farming country where I grew up—though it seemed more lush, perhaps more like the Midwest—when a group of farm women filed in and filled up the rest of the seats.

After I communicated to them that I didn't speak Polish, in response to their friendly inquiries, I huddled in the corner trying to catch a nap while they launched into animated conversation. A plump, jovial woman and a tall, gaunt woman with the eyes of a hawk sat across from each other at the center of the group, obviously the chief wits in an exchange of stories that had them all cracking up with laughter. Occasionally they would put their hands over their mouths and look over at me to see if I was listening, an indication I suspected that they were discussing things scandalous and perhaps sexual. I tried to suppress signs of my amusement, but felt myself shaking sometimes with contained laughter, which would elicit occasional suspicious glances.

I had no idea what they were talking about, but the way they laughed made me feel like everything in the world would be okay. Poland had just recently emerged from the long occupation by the Soviet Union, and I'd had numerous conversations about the prognosis for recovery from what for most had been a grim struggle since the beginning of World War II, one of many extended periods of occupation and resistance in the long history of their people. But laughter like this could heal not only Poland but the world, I thought, or at least help people to survive and even cherish hard times.

So when I got off the train in Poznan to prepare for my final lecture in Poland about the American myth of the frontier, I was still basking in the glow of that ride in a railroad car filled with laughter about stories in a language I could not fathom. I could easily imagine that the women I traveled with would have fit into that frontier world of my honyocker ancestors in northeastern Montana.

As I watched Mom and Helen laughing at our New Year's Eve party I wondered if this was part of a healing medicine that could never be entirely communicated in words, if something vital in this honyocker heritage might not be carried in laughter so deep that it wells up in tears.

And when Helen spoke of associating Mom with the image of the pioneer woman in "Song of the Lark," I also remembered my favorite old picture of Dad. It's a Xeroxed copy of the St. Labre Mission yearbook, on a page devoted to miscellaneous snapshots of students and the priests and nuns who taught there.

Dad sits cross-legged next to his saddle on the ground with his hat pushed back, looking like he just sat down to relax after a hard day's work, and the expression on his face intrigues me. He looks reflective and observant, with a bit of a wry smile forming by his lip and a glint in his eye, like someone who might say something perceptive and unexpected that would crack you up. He looks like a guy I can imagine cracking jokes and telling stories around a campfire. The picture has always made me wonder what he was really like back then, and what that old cowboy life was like, when they still slept out on the range in bedrolls, and they still ate meals around a chuck wagon during roundups.

He never seemed at all nostalgic for those old cowboy days, but I remember the pride he took in being a good hand at a time when the ability to wrangle horses and herd cattle and buck hay from dawn until night defined a man's worth. He changed a lot, I thought, looking back on his life.

His ranching heritage instilled in him some firm codes of manhood, which could be a source of strength but were not great at promoting flexibility. My sisters discussed how Mom found it difficult to adjust to expectations when they visited his ranching country, where to her men's and women's roles seemed so clearly separated. But Mom had been raised on a farm run by her mother, and women like Grossmutter Heisler and her aunt Gertie shared in decision-making as well as hard labor.

Dad could be hardheaded and difficult, and he maintained

firm control of the checkbook. But later in his life, especially after he quit drinking, he became comfortably and quite competently domestic in many ways. He'd been trained as a medic in the Navy and had at one time aspired to be a doctor, so he was actually an excellent nurse for my mother when she dealt with increasingly severe respiratory problems in their last years in Idaho. After his retirement he became a fine cook in his own right, branching out from the meat and potatoes fare that he'd cooked while Mom worked when he was in school, to baking the pies and homemade bread and rolls that always made eating at their home so special.

He'd always made occasional batches of homemade jellies and wine from chokecherries and buffalo berries when we had access to them, but in his later years he launched into large-scale canning operations. He filled shelves in the basement with jellies and jams and syrups and canned vegetables from his prolific fruit trees and garden, from which he constantly packed boxes of homegrown preserves in Mason jars to send home with visiting family and friends. He was a cowboy honyocker in the end, and my sisters claim that Mom felt her secret triumph in their marriage—which I doubt she would ever have taken credit for in front of him— was converting her ranching husband from being a Republican to a Democrat. The honyocker cowboy superintendent and the homesteader nurse—perhaps in the end, with all of their problems, they healed some old wounds as well.

After Mom's funeral I talked to Doris about how the family would change, and she observed, "Well, you know Kirk and Jill are talking about moving to Oregon." That would leave only Phil and his family here in Montana, I thought, and Montana had only really become the center of family

life again in those last years when the parents moved back
there. And now my brothers and sisters and I are the last
generation in our branch of the family to think of Montana
as home. The nephews and nieces are spread all over the
country, like us, and as of now we're not really a Montana
family anymore.

While I was driving west along the Hi-Line, sifting through
all the stories I'd gathered from southeastern and northeastern Montana, I had a vision of writing a new book recover-
ing the stories of those first generations, weaving together
stories converging from the four corners of Montana. In my
mind's eye I saw the Lynches from Ireland arriving in the
southeast by train in 1883, after my great-grandfather Lee
Tucker helped trail a cattle herd up from Nebraska to where
he would homestead with my great-grandmother Lena Lynch
down on Home Creek; Grossmutter Heisler's covered wagon
accompanied by kids and grandkids and farm animals wandering into the northeast from Canada in 1909; my great-
uncle Gene Ground's parents up in the northwest, surviving
those hard early reservation years up in Blackfeet country,
before my great-aunt Imelda married into the family; Marcus Daly arriving in the southwest mining camps from similar camps in California and Nevada to establish his copper
kingdom and hire my great-great-uncle Jack Lynch, who
would entice my great-great-grandparents Patrick and Margaret Lynch to migrate to the New World.

And so the saga of these first generations would describe
a great circle of the interwoven stories of all these families—
Irish, Blackfeet, Norwegian, German; cowboys, honyockers, miners, healers. I'll call it *Four Corners*, I thought, and
tell an epic story going back more than a century, about all

these peoples converging in this place we now call Montana to forge new lives or sustain the lives they had. But now I realized that, for my family, my parents' graves up by the Yellowstone River appear to conclude this version of a frontier story that still shapes our lives, often in ways we hardly recognize. My parents never owned a ranch or farm, so we have no specific family place that connects us to Montana. And here at the beginning of the twenty-first century we are dispersing again, as our ancestors did originally from near and far to converge in Montana.

Our heritage comes to us in many ways—as money and property; as old books and pictures we stow away believing some day we will know what to do with them; perhaps even as inherited debts and curses that have to be paid or exorcised. But most fundamentally our heritage comes to us through the stories we remember and create, both individually and collectively. Here at the beginning of a new millennium perhaps we in America especially need to preserve these stories of this generation that is passing away, this generation that witnessed the closing of frontiers that their parents and grandparents opened to them, that survived the Depression and shaped the world that we "Boomers"—a word that evokes this frontier tradition of boom and bust—were born into after the great war that changed them and the world.

And as we and our children and grandchildren enter this globalizing new world faced with challenges and opportunities and threats that previous generations could barely imagine, we must carry with us the stories we need—like the Lynches packing what they most cherished to take to their new home across the sea, or like Grossmutter Heisler saving her father's seeds from Minnesota for their homesteading journey, or like my great-uncle Gene's mother Mary Ground preserving the old oral story about Iniskim for its new life in a book.

We need hardship stories that tell us how to adapt to and survive unforeseen calamities. And perhaps most of all we need humor, tough-minded wit, to expose posturing and lies, and full-bodied laughter that restores our spirit and brings us to tears, reminding us that our deepest legacy is not about "conquering" the wilderness after all, but about being transformed by it and discovering it to be home. Perhaps we need to heal the wounds from shattered or displaced dreams of the past even as we envision new ones, savoring the passion and wisdom of the stories we inherit to help us create our own.

We must find and cherish medicine where we can, from the past or across cultures—to heal these old wounds, to preserve us in trials to come, to give us power to engage fully in our new stories as they unfold.

Bibliographical Essay

Having spent a career writing literary scholarship, I'm struck in retrospect by the variety of types of sources that have shaped this memoir. In a sense I suppose everything I've read informs these stories, but I'd like to acknowledge those specific texts that are either directly cited in my own book or that most influenced my understanding and interpretations.

Though their most important function may have been to inspire explanations and reminiscences from other family members, several local histories provided me with specific information and narratives that inform my stories. The most valuable references for reconstructing the ranching history of my father's family have been a memoir by my great-aunt Margaret Bailey Broadus, *Through the Rosebuds: Tales of Rosebud Creek, Montana* (1987), and, just recently, material written by family historian Cathy Byron in the program booklet for the Lynch-Callan Reunion, 2009. Also, a local history, *They Came and Stayed: Rosebud County History* (1977), provides colorful family stories and photographs.

Most useful in reconstructing the history of northeastern Montana were several other local histories: *Sheridan's Daybreak: A Story of Sheridan County and Its Pioneers* (1970), *Sheridan's Daybreak II* (1984), *Plentywood Portrait, Diamond Jubilee Book* (1987), and *Raymond Reflections, 1914–1989* (1990).

More general Montana histories that I have found useful include: G. B. Glasscock's *The War of the Copper Kings* (1935); Joseph Kinsley Howard's *Montana: High, Wide, and Handsome* (1943); Michael Malone's *The Battle for Butte: Mining and Politics on the Northern Frontier, 1864–1906* (1981); Jonathan Raban's *Bad Land: An American Romance* (1996); and *Montana: A History of Two Centuries*, by Michael P. Malone, et al. (second edition, 1999). Three classic books edited or written by Helena Huntington Smith originally inspired my interest in the cowboy era of southeastern Montana and northeastern Wyoming: E. C. "Teddy Blue" Abbott's memoir, *We Pointed Them North: Recollections of a Cowpuncher* (1939); Nannie Alderson's memoir, *A Bride Goes West* (1942); and *The War on Powder River: The History of an Insurrection* (1966).

I've been especially influenced by the rich heritage of writing about the West and Montana. Most specifically, my reflections have been inspired by classic western memoirs such as: *Wolf Willow* (1955), by Wallace Stegner; *The Blue Hen's Chick* (1965), by A. B. Guthrie; *This House of Sky* (1979), by Ivan Doig; *All But the Waltz* (1992), by Mary Clearman Blew; *Where Rivers Change Direction* (2000), by Mark Spragg; and *Breaking Clean* (2002), by Judy Blunt.

Most fundamentally, I suppose, my interpretations of Montana heritage have been shaped by fiction, beginning with classic novels that define the western literary tradition, such as Owen Wister's *The Virginian* (1902), Willa Cather's *My Antonia* (1918), and A. B. Guthrie Jr.'s *The Big Sky* (1947). William W. Bevis's *Ten Tough Trips: Montana Writers and the West* (1990) provides an interesting interpretation of Montana literary traditions for anyone interested in an overview of the material. In more contemporary fiction I was especially inspired by Norman Maclean's *A River Runs Through*

It (1976), with its vivid, poetic reconstruction of the Montana world that Mclean left behind as a young man. James Welch's highly acclaimed series of novels provide the most in-depth literary interpretation of the central Hi-Line region, primarily from a Native American point of view: *Winter in the Blood* (1974); *The Death of Jim Loney* (1979); *Fools Crow* (1986); and *The Indian Lawyer* (1990).

Of special interest for this project are books dealing specifically with eastern Montana, so I was gratified to discover the only novel I know that casts a "honyocker" as the western hero, Giles A. Lutz's *The Honyocker* (1961), winner of the Silver Spur Award in 1962. There is now an expanding tradition of fiction about this region. Some of the most memorable novels include Mildred Walker's *Winter Wheat* (1944), Ivan Doig's *Bucking the Sun* (1996), and Larry Watson's *Montana 1948* (1993) and *White Crosses* (1997). An excellent new history focuses specifically on radical politics during the homesteading era in the Plentywood area: Verlaine Stoner McDonald's *The Red Corner: The Rise and Fall of Communism in Northeastern Montana* (2010).

Finally, the Internet provides useful sources of information and commentary about relevant subjects such as the Montana Hi-Line and the term "honyocker." I recommend to anyone with interests in these topics that they explore the electronic frontier of information.